CLASSROO MENT
FOR SCHO

D0406587

Editor

William S. Bush

Case Editors

Mary Bennion

Lise Dworkin

Lew Romagnano

Carolyn Ronchinsky

Mathematics Assessment

Cases and Discussion Questions

FOR GRADES 6-12

NATIONAL COUNCIL
OF TEACHERS OF
MATHEMATICS
RESTON, VIRGINIA

Library of Congress Cataloging-in-Publication Data

Mathematics assessment : cases and discussion questions for grades 6–12 / editor William S. Bush.
    p. cm. — (Classroom assessment for school mathematics K–12)
  Includes bibliographical references and index.
  ISBN 0-87353-482-4
  1. Mathematics—Study and teaching (Middle school)—United States—Evaluation. 2. Mathematics—Study and teaching (Secondary)—United States—Evaluation. 3. Mathematical ability—Testing. I. Bush, William S. II. Series.

QA13 .M1533 2000
510′.71′273—dc21

00-061620

Printed in the United States of America

Mathematics
Assessment

Cases and Discussion Questions

FOR GRADES 6-12

Table of Contents

ACKNOWLEDGMENTS

We wish to thank the follow educators for contributing cases to this book. Without their willingness to share part of their teaching lives with us, this book would not have been possible.

Jodi Anderson	Peggy Kirk
Mary Bennion	Richard Kitchen
Julia Burns	Jennifer Mackiney
Duncan Chui	Ingrid Oyen
Donna Clauson	Lew Romagnano
Sheila Conry	Rheta Rubenstein
Deanna De'Liberto	Marcia Seeley
Gloria Dion	Sandy Siegel
Holly Drier	Sue Stetzer
Joseph Garofalo	Sandy Wilcox

We wish to thank Judith Olsen and Stephanie Robinson, who encouraged teachers taking their university classes to submit stories about their assessment experiences. We also wish to thank Lise Dworkin of the San Francisco Unified School District for working with teachers to write assessment cases. Her initial editing of these cases made our work easier.

We would like to thank Carne Barnett of WestEd, who served as a consultant to this project from the outset. Her expertise in helping teachers write cases, and in helping us edit cases and think about how to use cases in professional development, proved invaluable.

We wish to thank Katherine Merseth, Joan Karp, and Carolyn Ronchinsky of the Harvard Mathematics Case Development Project for sharing their expertise in case writing. Their advice helped us shape cases that would be useful to teachers.

We wish to thank Deborah Bryant of the Education Development Center for sharing her expertise in writing, revising, and facilitating cases. Her expertise in writing and revising cases, and in building professional development programs based on cases, improved the quality of our work.

THE ASSESSMENT ADDENDA TASK FORCE

William S. Bush, *Chair*

Charles Allen

Florence Glanfield

Anja S. Greer

Steve Leinwand

Jean Kerr Stenmark

Dear Reader,

The National Council of Teachers of Mathematics asked our task force to create an addenda series to support the Assessment Standards for School Mathematics. *This book, one of six books in the series, describes real activities, students, and teachers in assessment situations in grades 6–12 classrooms. It also includes reflective questions to encourage discussion about important issues in assessment. In addition, four Practical Handbooks for teachers in grades K–2, 3–5, 6–8, and 9–12 contain practical examples and ideas from teachers who have been successful with assessment. The final book in the series presents assessment cases from grades K–5 classrooms.*

The Assessment Standards *tells us that classroom assessment should—*

■ *provide a rich variety of mathematical topics and problem situations;*

■ *give students opportunities to investigate problems in many ways;*

■ *question and listen to students;*

■ *look for evidence of learning from many sources;*

■ *expect students to use concepts and procedures effectively in solving problems.*

The examples, reflections, explanations, and tips are intended to help all of us explore the role of assessment in reshaping mathematics teaching and learning. We know that assessment, from simple observations to standardized tests, has always affected what we do in the classroom. We looked for examples that might help us do a better job so that we can have a better idea of what we really want students to learn.

We also know that classrooms and schools are complex places. Changing assessment practices in nonsupportive environments is challenging at best. We will share the experiences and stories of teachers who have had some success. We also will share the stories of teachers who have struggled with assessment.

Many people contributed to this effort. Classroom teachers and teacher educators shared their stories in this book to get us to reflect on our practices and beliefs about assessment, teaching, and learning.

This book, Cases and Discussion Questions for Grades 6–12, *is divided into an introduction and four chapters. The introduction explains what cases are and what their purposes are. Chapters 1, 2, and 3 discuss cases about using new assessment approaches, cases about scoring assessment, and cases about using assessment results. The final chapter, "Facilitator Guidelines and Notes," gives guidelines for working through each assessment case. At the end of the book, we have provided a bibliography of further reading and an index to help you locate topics of greatest interest to you.*

We hope you will find many uses for this series. Enjoy!

—*The Assessment Addenda Task Force*

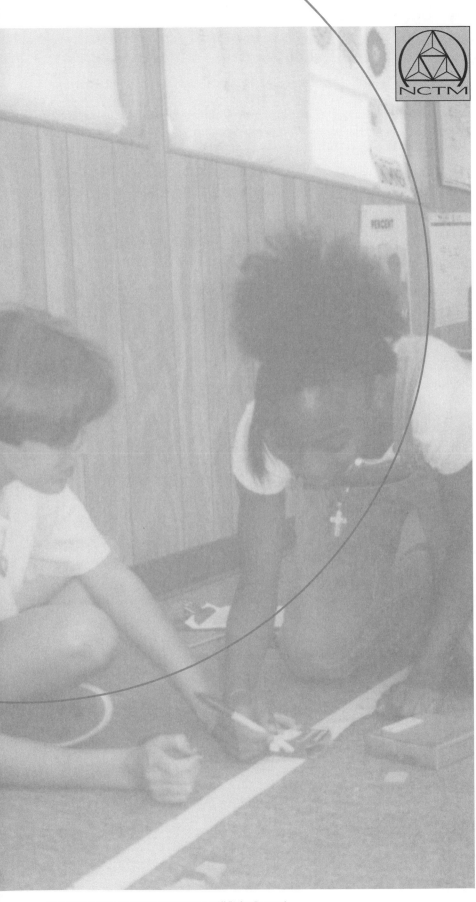

Mathematics Assessment: Cases and Discussion Questions for Grades 6–12

Photograph by the Goudy/Schleicher Group: All Rights Reserved.

Introduction

The National Council of Teachers of Mathematics provides a vision of classroom assessment that will enable us to assess the full mathematics power of our students. This vision is reflected through recommendations in the Evaluation section of the *Curriculum and Evaluation Standards for School Mathematics* and through the *Assessment Standards for School Mathematics*.

The *Assessment Standards* shares six standards to guide us:

Standard 1: Assessment should reflect the mathematics that all students need to know and be able to do.

Standard 2: Assessment should enhance mathematics learning.

Standard 3: Assessment should promote equity.

Standard 4: Assessment should be an open process.

Standard 5: Assessment should promote valid inferences about mathematics learning.

Standard 6: Assessment should be a coherent process.

Meeting these standards might require significant changes in our assessment practices. **Figure A** outlines a set of shifts in practices that must occur if we are to meet these standards for classroom assessment.

FIG. A

MAJOR SHIFTS IN ASSESSMENT PRACTICE (from National Council of Teachers of Mathematics [NCTM] 1995, p. 83)

TOWARD	AWAY FROM
■ Assessing students' full mathematical power	■ Assessing only students' knowledge of specific facts and isolated skills
■ Comparing students' performance with established criteria	■ Comparing students' performance with that of other students
■ Giving support to teachers and credence to their informed judgment	■ Designing "teacher-proof" assessment systems
■ Making the assessment process public, participatory, and dynamic	■ Making the assessment process secret, exclusive, and fixed
■ Giving students multiple opportunities to demonstrate their full mathematical power	■ Restricting students to a single way of demonstrating their mathematical knowledge
■ Developing a shared vision of what to assess and how to do it	■ Developing assessment by oneself
■ Using assessment results to ensure that all students have the opportunity to achieve their potential	■ Using assessment to filter and select students out of the opportunities to learn mathematics
■ Aligning assessment with curriculum and instruction	■ Treating assessment as independent of curriculum or instruction
■ Basing inferences on multiple sources of evidence	■ Basing inferences on restricted or single sources of evidence
■ Viewing students as active participants in the assessment process	■ Viewing students as the objects of assessment
■ Regarding assessment as continual and recursive	■ Regarding assessment as sporadic and conclusive
■ Holding all concerned with mathematics learning accountable for assessment results	■ Holding only a few accountable for assessment results

Introduction

Making important shifts in assessment practice is a difficult task. The result, however, will be a clearer picture of what our students know about mathematics, what they can do with mathematics, and how they think mathematically. Using a variety of valid, reliable assessment tools can help us understand and communicate to others the mathematics power our students hold.

We have found that the best way to learn about assessment and to make changes in practices is through working with other teachers. Listening to teachers talk about their experiences, watching other teachers at work, and working beside colleagues show us ways to learn new approaches. By doing so, we are often challenged to question practices we or other teachers have used over the years.

For these reasons, NCTM developed *Mathematics Assessment: Cases and Discussion Questions for Grades 6–12* as a professional development tool both for teachers who want to change their assessment practices and for teachers who have struggled with changes over the years. This book gives a glimpse into the assessment experiences of middle school and high school mathematics teachers around the continent. Through these cases, we hope you will reflect on your own assessment practices and analyze your beliefs about assessment, teaching, and learning. In discussing these cases with others, we hope you will learn strategies to improve your classroom assessment practices.

WHAT ARE CASES ABOUT ASSESSMENT?

The cases in this book are stories written by mathematics teachers or other educators describing experiences with classroom assessment. They were designed to raise issues and pose dilemmas about assessment.

WHAT ARE THE PURPOSES OF CASES ABOUT ASSESSMENT?

These cases are professional development tools designed to—

- ■ stimulate reflection about assessment practices;
- ■ explore issues about classroom assessment;
- ■ encourage the examination of beliefs about classroom assessment.

As a professional development tool, they have several advantages:

- ■ They allow us to analyze teaching and assessment practices carefully and respectfully.
- ■ They allow us to analyze and solve teaching problems collaboratively.
- ■ They allow us to bring our own meanings and experiences to each problem or dilemma.
- ■ They model classroom teaching where students must analyze and solve problems on their own.
- ■ They help us build a repertoire of strategies for resolving difficult classroom dilemmas.
- ■ They expose us to many different points of view about assessment.

Introduction

HOW DO I USE THIS BOOK?

This book is intended to be used as a professional development tool for mathematics teachers in grades 6–12. It is appropriate for beginning teachers as well as teachers with experience—including those who have tried many different types of classroom assessment. We believe we can learn from the discussions sparked by the situations presented in these cases.

We suggest that the cases be read and discussed in groups. You can use the assessment cases here as a professional development experience in themselves. They may also supplement professional development workshops that focus on assessment strategies.

We can use the assessment cases in teacher preparation courses to help prospective teachers learn about mathematics assessment and the issues that surround it. Student teachers and their cooperating teachers can read and discuss the cases as a means to understand each other's assessment practices and beliefs.

Finally, we can use the cases for individual professional growth. Simply sitting down and reading the cases alone may provide insight into our own assessment practices. If you use the cases in this manner, however, we recommend that you read the facilitator notes along with the cases to stimulate reflection about a wide range of issues.

WHERE CAN I FIND OTHER CASES ABOUT MATHEMATICS ASSESSMENT?

Fractions, Decimals, Ratios, & Percents: Hard to Learn and Hard to Teach, by Carne Barnett, Donna Goldenstein, and Babette Jackson, offers twenty-nine cases written about learning and teaching rational numbers. Many of these cases focus on important issues about classroom assessment. A facilitator guide for leading discussions about the cases is sold separately.

Cases of Secondary Mathematics Classrooms, by Katherine Merseth and Joan Karp of the Harvard Mathematics Case Development Project, includes twenty written cases from high school mathematics classrooms. Although cases focus on mathematics, instructional issues, and students' thinking, many cases also address important issues of assessment. Notes included in the book will help facilitate discussions about the cases.

Casebook of School Reform, edited by Barbara Miller and Ilene Kantrov, offers cases about school reform. Some cases focus on mathematics and assessment.

Mathematics Assessment: A Video Library, K–12 was produced by the Educational Programming Group of the WGBH Educational Foundation. It includes six video cases, complete with classroom action followed by teacher reflection. It comes with a guidebook for using the videos in professional development experiences.

Chapter 1

Cases about Using New Assessment Approaches

Tessellation Presentation

Last year, I developed a tessellation project for my seventh-grade students to assess their understanding of six key geometric concepts: symmetry, congruence, similarity, reflections, slides, and rotations. My students enjoyed the project very much. Every student was able to make a tessellation. The open-ended nature of this project allowed for creativity and different degrees of complexity in the designs. But I have been hesitant to try this project again. Why? Well, first, this project took a lot of time. Second, I am not sure exactly what the students learned from the project. Did it warrant the amount of time given to it?

The more I thought about this project, the more I remembered the enthusiasm that the students showed. It was a lot of work on my part, but maybe it was worth it. Perhaps I had learned more about the students through this project than I remembered. Perhaps they benefited in ways I had not intended.

THE TESSELLATION PROJECT

The project began as an attempt to enliven my unit on geometry. I was disappointed with my previous units on geometry. They seemed to emphasize and assess just vocabulary. I looked through my mathematics book for ideas. Suddenly it occurred to me that I had some materials about tessellations. They might be engaging and fun. Students could be creative and make their own patterns, like M. C. Escher, or could use pattern blocks to create designs. Furthermore, I could easily assess students' understanding of geometric concepts. Students could grasp important concepts like congruent and similar figures concretely. I could also assess their ability to use the various forms of transformations, such as slides, rotations, and reflections. This was perfect! All these ideas could be built into a tessellation.

The unit began, as my past units had, with the development of vocabulary. We used geoboards to create figures. We used dot paper to draw congruent and similar figures, as well as to show examples of symmetry, rotations, reflections, and slides. Next, I used a handout to describe what I expected from the students in the project. I asked students to create tessellations that incorporated the six concepts we had studied. The tessellations were to be drawn neatly and colored in a way that would make it easy to identify the concepts. At the end of the unit, students gave a short presentation in front of the class about the concepts illustrated in their tessellations. They were also responsible for evaluating each other's tessellations. I even created a checklist to help students assess the presentations. (See **fig. 1.1.**) Their overall grade depended on their tessellation, their presentation, and their evaluations of their fellow students' presentations.

We spent the next few days in the computer lab with a program called Exploring Math with Manipulatives: Reflecting on Patterns. Several activities explored symmetry and reflections. In one section, students had to manipulate pattern blocks and create designs by rotating or reflecting the pattern blocks. I encouraged students to explore on their own and create tessellations that could be drawn for their final project. Since we did not have color printers and the printouts were small, students eventually had to draw and color their designs by hand.

Tessellation Presentation

ASSESSING THEIR PROGRESS

I also encouraged students to use correct vocabulary as they shared their ideas with each other. I listened closely to their animated discussions and recorded my observations on a checklist. (See **fig. 1.1**.)

FIG. 1.1

TESSELLATION CHECKLIST

Student	congruent figures	similar figures	rotation	reflection	slide	symmetry

Tessellation checklist

Tessellation Presentation

If students correctly identified one of the six concepts without any help, I gave them 5 points. I gave 3 points to those students needing clarification. I wrote down some of the dialogue I overheard. In reviewing their comments, I noticed that some students were learning the six concepts:

Wendy:	Look, Jane. I have four things built into my pattern. Here's a rotation. See, it turns from here to there. Here're reflection and congruent figures. And this one slides from here to here.
Joe:	Ms. Cloyd, how can we build similar figures?
Ms. Cloyd:	That's a good question. Does anyone have an idea that might help Joe?
Jane:	Yes, I did it! You can arrange four triangles to make one that is two lengths on each side so that your big triangle is similar to the small one, because the angles are still the same. The sides are just twice as long.
Ms. Cloyd:	Very good. Are there any other shapes that would work?
Raphael:	Yes, I built it with the squares. It works the same as the triangles.
Anika:	I did it with the blue blocks. It's a rhombus, I think, yes, that's it. A rhombus.

I continued around the room and checked to see if every student could identify the concepts in their pictures. They explained to me where each concept occurred, and I recorded it on my checklist.

PRESENTATION DAY

The day for presentations arrived. I set up the video camera and passed out checklists to each student. The checklists, similar to the one I used in the computer lab, included a place for everyone's name and the six concepts. I asked students to check the concepts as class members made their presentations. I also asked them to write comments on the back explaining why they disagreed with concepts shown by other students. At this stage I used a point-based evaluation form for each student. (See **fig. 1.2.**) Later, I compared my evaluations of each presenter with the evaluations from other students. If students recognized mistakes made by others, I felt that they had a good grasp on the concepts. If not, I believed that they probably had only a partial understanding of the concepts.

Tessellation Presentation

FIG. 1.2

TESSELLATION PROJECT EVALUATION SHEET

Evaluation of Tessellation Project

Each of the six concepts was apparent in the tessellation, and the oral presentation demonstrated an understanding of each concept listed below.

Concept	Points Possible	Points Earned
1. Congruent figures	10	_____
2. Similar figures	10	_____
3. Translation (slide)	10	_____
4. Reflection	10	_____
5. Rotation	10	_____
6. Symmetry	10	_____
7. Pattern is apparent	10	_____
8. Covers entire posterboard	5	_____
9. Neatly drawn	5	_____
10. Neatly colored	5	_____
11. Size equals 12″ × 15″	5	_____
12. Appropriate voice clarity, projection, and speed	10	_____

Total Possible = 100 Points

Total Earned = _____

Letter Grade = _____

Tessellation Presentation

THE RESULTS

I was delighted with both the presentations and evaluations. It was obvious that the students were very proud of their beautiful tessellations. In addition, they were very complimentary of each other's work. Most of the students commented how creative or neat the projects were. I was very pleased with how engaged they were in the evaluation process.

Most students had learned the six concepts very well, gaining a much deeper understanding of these geometric concepts than they had in past years. I also got a better sense of what they understood through their presentations and evaluations. This assessment, however, had definite limitations. It took a very long time to get to students in the computer lab and for them to describe and demonstrate each concept to me. Even after interviewing students, I was sometimes uncertain if they really understood the concepts. For example, if the tessellating figure was a regular polygon, it was impossible to tell the difference among slides, reflections, or rotations. When students used regular polygons in their designs, I could not assess whether they understood the distinction among the different transformations. I also noticed that some students had difficulty in coloring their designs to highlight congruent figures. Did these students really understand congruence? Doubts about what the students actually learned crept into my mind. It took a lot of time to plan and implement this assessment. I wonder how I might get more evidence about what they really understand when I use this task again.

CHAPTER *1*

Does It Measure Up?

Approaching the unit on measurement once again, I took a look at last year's plan book and grimaced. The unit on measurement in my seventh-grade classes has continuously produced less than satisfactory results from my students. I basically taught a single lesson from the textbook, which required minimal measuring. Only six out of a total of twenty-two questions in the book asked students to actually measure something. In fact, most questions asked for historical facts about the development of standardized measurement systems. In class, we read the lesson together and did the problems in the back. The accompanying homework assignment also included very little actual measuring. What students did measure, they measured at home. It was difficult for me to tell where students had trouble with measuring. Grades on the assignments were never very good. This was the year to make a change.

MY NEW MEASUREMENT LESSON

I began my new lesson by having my students examine rulers and meter-sticks. We quickly reviewed the names for the markings in both the customary and the metric systems. I knew these students had learned about measurement in science class, since the science teacher and I worked together to avoid an overlap of curriculum. I had two goals: (1) they needed to learn to measure objects, and (2) they needed to become good estimators. I hoped that without too much preparation, the class would be ready to participate in my new measurement activity.

I established nine "stations" at various locations in the room. The stations contained familiar classroom items: the height of the statue on the shelf, the teacher's desk, and the snowman on the bulletin board; the length of the window in the door, a paper clip, the mirror hanging in the room, and a cork strip; and the width of the thermometer casing and the work table. Through measuring objects students see every day, I hoped that they would learn some concrete guidelines for reasonable estimates of these objects.

Does It Measure Up?

The students chose a partner; I assigned each of the nine pairs to a station. I distributed a meterstick with customary units on the reverse side and a chart to record results (see **fig. 1.3**) to each pair.

"At each station, you are to measure each item in customary and metric units," I explained to the class. "Both partners are to measure and then decide on a measurement that seems appropriate. I will allow three minutes at each station. I will say 'move to the next station' at the end of that time, and you will advance to the station at your right. Before we begin, are there any questions?"

"Mrs. Martens, do we have to measure in metric?" Matt blurted out. "I don't like using it—it's too confusing." Looking around the room, I could tell that most students felt uncomfortable with the idea of measuring in metric. "Yes, you have to measure in metric," I replied. "Just remember what we discussed about the relationship of each unit in metric and what you learned in science."

FIG. 1.3

MEASUREMENT OBJECTS

Item	#1	#2	#3	#4	#5	#6	#7	#8	#9	
Angel										
Thermom.										
Desk										
Table										
Window										
Paper Clip										
Mirror										
Snowman										
Cork Strip										

Does It Measure Up?

STUDENTS HARD AT WORK

The students went to work. As the students moved from station to station, I watched and listened to each pair measure and then record their results. As an observer, I liked that I was available for questions that arose. The two questions that students asked most frequently were, "Which side are the centimeters?" and "Can we use this (holding a meterstick) as a yard?" Instead of providing answers, I tried to rephrase the question by asking, "How could you figure out on your own if I weren't here to help you?" Usually, this response began a discussion between partners with an occasional consultation with another group to find an answer. All the pairs resolved their own questions, and the class continued to determine the size of the object at their station.

CLASS RESULTS

After everyone rotated through all stations, the pairs recorded the class results on a big chart drawn on the board. Students quickly discovered some differences in the results:

Maria: Hey! How can the first group have a measurement for the cork strip of 1 meter and 18 1/2 inches? They can't combine the two systems, can they?"

Nathan: Mike and Jay have some fifths and sevenths for their measurements. Our ruler isn't divided into those fractions. Where did they get those fractions?

Allison: Why are all of Katie's and Jane's measurements in decimals? That is too confusing when the rest of us have used fractions!

Without prompting, the students asked important questions. As they continued to record results on the master chart, I was impressed by their focus and determination. I did not have to discipline anyone for being off task. Once the class chart was complete, I decided to revisit the questions they had raised. I asked students to help me find the answers.

Sabrina began by commenting on Maria's question about combining the two systems, "The measurements need to be in the same system—either metric or customary. They can't be half in one and half in the other. The first group should either change the meter to feet or the inches to centimeters."

Does It Measure Up?

After some discussion about Sabrina's comments, the class agreed with her. I asked the class to help the first group correct their measurements by changing 1 meter to feet or by changing 18 1/2 inches to centimeters. Several students volunteered answers, and as a group, we chose to write the answer in metric units.

> **Jacob:** Mike and Jay counted the tick marks instead of looking at the spaces between. Maybe that's where they got odd numbers for denominators.

> **Cassie:** Yeah, the six-sevenths is probably supposed to be six-eighths!

I asked for a volunteer to review customary markings on the ruler. A few hands went up, and I called on Matt, who seemed to have a good grasp of the customary system. He approached the board and drew an enlarged inch. He then divided the inch using proper marking for eighths, including the correct labels. After watching Matt, Mike acknowledged that he and Jay had been confused. They both wanted to remeasure to correct any wrong measurements.

> **Teacher:** What about Katie's and Jane's decimals?

> **Jacob:** Well, they're not wrong, just confusing, because everyone else used fractions.

> **Teacher:** How do you know they're not wrong?

> **Maggie:** We really don't know if they're wrong because we don't know what the fraction was that they changed to a decimal. If the fraction was 3/4, then it would be right.

We then discussed "how much" a fraction is compared to a whole and how that equal decimals should represent the same amount as the fraction. To check the measurement, we wrote the decimal exactly as it is said in words and then put it into fraction form. The students then reduced the fraction. Some students had trouble with the conversion process, so I asked the class to help Katie and Jane change all their decimals to fractions as a reinforcement activity. It is always surprising to me how many junior high school students cannot do this, but by the end of the list, most students seemed comfortable with the process. Afterwards, I asked Katie and Jane to remeasure the items to see the measurement for themselves.

Does It Measure Up?

WRAP-UP DISCUSSION

Ready to begin the wrap-up discussion, I told them that their input into solving the few problems that some groups faced was very helpful. However, I asked if anyone noticed anything in particular about the problems that had to be fixed. Was there a common pattern? I paused a moment, and a bunch of hands went up.

Kevin: Well, I noticed that all the things we had to fix were in the customary measurement.

Teacher: I noticed the same thing. Why do you think there were no problems with the metric system?

Calvin: The metric system is really easier to use because everything is in tenths. You just add the number of tenths and write it as a decimal. The customary is a lot more work if you have to reduce fractions or do any adding!

Looking around the room, I noticed several other students nodded in agreement (even Matt).

This concluded the measurement activity, and students passed in their charts to be graded. As the students got ready to go to their next class, I listened to them discuss the events of the past two days in math class—they clearly liked the change of pace.

Flipping through their work, I could see that their charts were accurate and complete. I began developing several extension activities using the information that we had already gathered. I planned to find class averages for each station tomorrow and then find area and perimeter using our measurement skills. Sitting back at my desk, I realized that I had enjoyed the new way of learning about measurement too. Not only had the students been exposed to hands-on experiences with measurement in metric and customary systems, but they had reviewed fractions and decimals as well—topics the text had not touched at all in the lesson.

Does It Measure Up?

STUDENTS' COMMENTS ABOUT THE ACTIVITY

At the end of each year, I asked students to tell me the lessons and activities that they liked and disliked. I also asked suggestions for next year's seventh-grade math class. Here are some of the comments students made this year:

> I don't really like working out of the book much because it is hard to understand and it is very boring. I really liked the measurement activity, and you should do it again. I also liked doing angles. I don't like doing algebra very much.

> I like working out of the book; it isn't as confusing. I think you should keep the measuring game. I really disliked doing fractions.

> What activities! I think you should do problem solving; you should also do the measurement because a lot of people enjoyed it.

> Liked: measurement activity and problem solving. I LOVED doing graphs.

NOW WHAT?

In reviewing students' comments, I saw that every student believed that the measurement activity should be kept! I realize that using new instruction and assessment is a guessing game—sometimes it works and sometimes it doesn't. What was most valuable for me in this lesson was that I knew students knew about mathematics. I could tell if they understood how to measure, if they could use different units, and if they could use fractions and decimals. This information had not been available to me in the textbook exercises. Furthermore, I found out what they knew before giving them a test or quiz.

I have a real problem now. I am hooked on this way of teaching and assessing students. My experiment was a real success, and I want to change all my mathematics lessons to be like this one. But I don't know how. I am stuck with this old textbook for another two years. Where can I get the resources? Whom can I ask for help? Where can I find the time?

CHAPTER *1*

Open Car Wash

In November my sixth-grade gifted and talented students finished a five-week unit on large numbers. The students worked in small groups to figure out how long it would take to collect and count one million bottle caps. They used a map to see how far they would have to hike if they took one million paces. They computed the height of a stack of one billion and one trillion pieces of paper. I now wanted to know what they could do individually with the concept of numbers like a million. I found a task that I felt would give me some information about each child's ability to handle large numbers.

THE OPEN-ENDED TASK

A car wash advertises that they have millions of satisfied customers each year. Is this reasonable?

I presented the task to the class. The instant chatter told me that I had caught their attention and interest. After a few minutes of general discussion, I asked them to list what a quality piece of work should contain. They came up with standard guidelines that we had been using weekly since September:

■ Show how you solved the problem.

■ Make sure you label all numbers.

■ Make sure someone can understand your thinking.

QUESTIONS, QUESTIONS, QUESTIONS

I then asked them if they had any questions before beginning the task. Hands shot up!

"How many hours will the car wash be open?"

"How long does it take to wash a car?"

"How big is the car wash?"

The questions tumbled out. I explained that I did not have any information. They were going to have to make some assumptions. I explained that students would have to make their own decisions about any unknowns. "You mean that I can have the car wash open for twenty-four hours a day?" inquired Ben. "That's fine," I replied. I again told the class that they would have to let the reader know their decisions.

The class became quiet as they got into the problem. A few minutes passed. One by one my students came to me with many questions:

"Can a car wash be open every day of the year?"

"Is it okay to have a car wash take ten minutes?"

"How many cars can be washed at a time?"

Open Car Wash

CONCERNS ABOUT THE TASK

In my mind I began to question the task. Was it too open? Should I have given them some suggestions on how to set limits? Previously I gave them several problems where they were required to add their own reasonable interpretations. Students presented their solutions to the class and had to explain their decisions. I gave them positive verbal and written responses to their solutions and pointed out to the class the variety of responses that an open-ended problem has. Why were they having trouble now?

I decided to respond to their individual questions by encouraging them to state their decision in their work. "Sure, just let the reader know what you decided." "Make sure you put that down in your solution." "Whatever you decide, just let the reader know."

STUDENTS' WORK

After about thirty minutes students began turning in their solutions. I glanced at some of them. Jamie wrote down a lot of questions. He did some calculations. He had made a decision, but what had I learned from this piece of work? (See **fig. 1.4**.)

FIG. 1.4

OPEN CAR WASH: STUDENT'S WORK #1

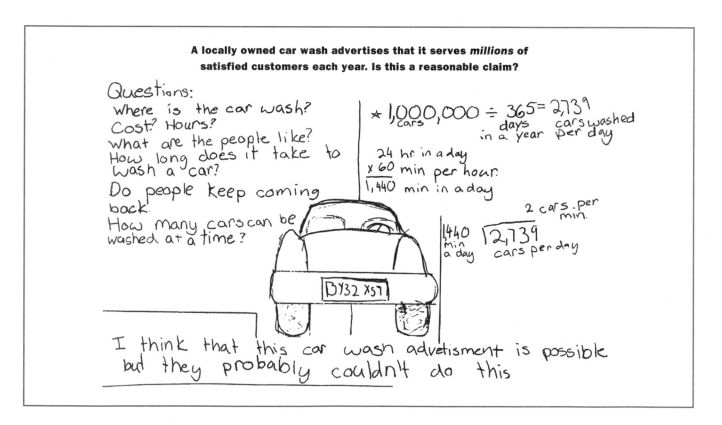

A locally owned car wash advertises that it serves *millions* of satisfied customers each year. Is this a reasonable claim?

Questions:
Where is the car wash?
Cost? Hours?
What are the people like?
How long does it take to wash a car?
Do people keep coming back.
How many cars can be washed at a time?

$1,000,000 \div 365 = 2,739$
cars / days / cars washed in a year per day

24 hr in a day
× 60 min per hour
1,440 min in a day

2 cars per min.

1,440 min a day) 2,739 cars per day

I think that this car wash advetisment is possible but they probably couldn't do this

CHAPTER *1*

Open Car Wash

FURTHER REFLECTION

After looking at Mark's solution, I was left with more questions: What was I really assessing with this type of question? How can I improve my students' understanding of what types of interpretations they need to make in answering open-ended questions? (See **fig. 1.5**.)

FIG. 1.5

OPEN CAR WASH: STUDENT'S WORK #2

I don't think it is reasonable because each day the car wash has to wash 2,739 cars. Besides no one has a car that is so dirty. I see people in the Sunset District park their cars in front of their house, take out a bucket of soapy water and wash their car themselves. This is what I did to get 2739 cars needed wash each day.

1,000,000 cars each year washed as a claim
$\div$ 365 days
———
2,739 cars needed to be washed each day

Let's say it opens 7 days a week. It is open 24 hours a day.

In a hour the carwash needs to wash 114 cars.

2,739 cars needed to wash a day
$\div$ 24 hours
———
114 cars needed to wash in a hour

This is a chart of what vehicle and how long it takes to wash

Vehicle	Time of Wash
Vans	12 mins
Trucks	9 mins
Sedans	8 mins
Compact Cars	5 mins
Wagons	10 mins
Sport Cars A bit larger than compacts	6 mins
Old Times Cars	7 mins

Max. (approx.)

In 1 minute the wash needs about 2 cars washed.

114 cars needed to wash in a hour
$\div$ 60 mins.
———
1.9 cars need to wash in a minute
Round off (2.0)

Suppose a whole derby of compact cars went to the car wash. In a minute 2 cars or needed to be washed. It takes 5 minutes to wash and dry the car. 2 cars × 5 mins = 10 mins of time to wash 2 cars (compact).

Where Did That Question Come From?

As part of a staff development project in my school district, I met regularly with fellow middle school mathematics teachers. Our objectives were to identify good assessment tasks and to look at students' responses. We selected what we thought were good assessment tasks, gave them to our seventh-grade students, and brought back samples of our students' work. We hoped that we would be able to judge the effectiveness of the assessment task and determine what "quality work" looked like. Although our deadline to give the area and perimeter task to the students came in the middle of a unit on perimeter and area, I believed my students were adequately prepared. I was eager to see just what they understood about these concepts.

THE TASK

The task asked students to draw all possible rectangles that have a perimeter of 18 units. That was just the takeoff point, however. Next, the task asked more challenging questions about maximizing the area for any given perimeter. Before my students even attempted that part, however, I was presented with a dilemma.

CONFUSION

I gave the task to my seventh-grade class. Soon after students began working on it, Jackie, a capable and conscientious student who I thought had grasped the ideas quite well, came to me for clarification. She showed me her work and asked, "Should I count the dots around the edge?" (See **fig. 1.6.**)

FIG. 1.6

JACKIE'S WORK

In the space below, show all the four-sided corral designs Tim can make with 18 units of fence. Label them so that Tim can see which one has the biggest area.

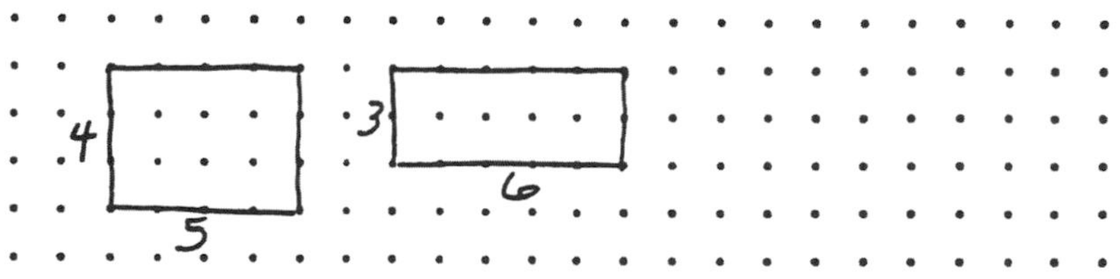

Where Did That Question Come From?

I was very surprised by her confusion. She had many experiences measuring various shapes, regular and irregular, using string and tape measures for perimeter and square tiles for area. In previous investigations, she used square grid paper or plain paper to draw all possible rectangles with a given perimeter or a given area. Although I had never given her dot paper, I felt Jackie knew the difference between linear and square units. I hoped that she would resolve the problem once she tried to find the areas of the rectangles. But here she was, asking me to help her.

Should I make a simple clarification, like "No, don't count the dots; count the spaces between the dots"? Or, should I provide a gentle reminder to shift her thinking, like "Remember how we measured perimeter with string?" Or, should I ask leading questions, like "How would you draw a 2 by 7 rectangle?" or "What about a 1 by 8 rectangle?" Or, should I provide her with grid paper or plain paper that she had used in previous activities that would eliminate the distraction the dot paper was creating? Should I tell her that I am not allowed to help her during this assessment?

By coincidence, my fellow mathematics teachers who met regularly were also evaluating this task with their classes. It was important for us to know if this task created confusion for some students. If it interfered with their ability to show what they understood about area and perimeter, then the task would not be effective.

With this in mind, I said, "Jackie, I want to understand your thinking. Please explain as best you can how you are solving this problem." She went away still confused and a little frustrated. Several other students came up to me and asked similar questions. Now I was really puzzled.

UNDERSTANDING THE CONFUSION

That night, I kept thinking about the difficulty that some of my students had with this task. With all the work we had done in class, how could these students be stumped by the dot paper? Then I remembered two previous activities that might have inadvertently misled students and interfered with their understanding of perimeter.

Where Did That Question Come From?

The first activity in my measurement unit asked students to draw several designs for patios with different areas using a given number of evenly spaced plants as a border. (See **fig. 1.7**.)

FIG. 1.7

PATIO PROBLEM

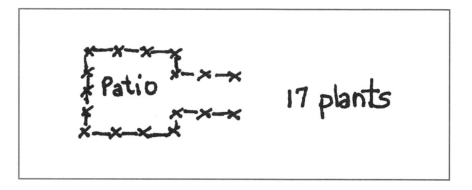

Students spent time drawing patios with decorative plants, being sure to count the plants to meet the requirements stated in the problem. It never occurred to me to discuss the difference between counting the plants and measuring the perimeter. Maybe Jackie counted dots as if they were plants.

Where Did That Question Come From?

Much earlier in the year, before the unit on area and perimeter, students investigated how many squares were on the border of a 10 by 10 grid. (See **fig. 1.8.**) Although students gave written explanations for six different methods of determining how many border squares there were for different sized square grids, it might also have led to some confusion with the concept of perimeter. A 10 by 10 grid has 36 border squares, but it has a perimeter of 40 units.

FIG. 1.8

SQUARES ON 10 × 10 BORDER

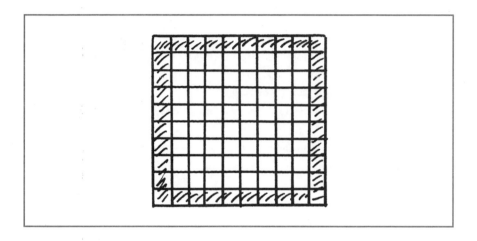

Perhaps these two investigations might have created some confusion about perimeter. If so, what adjustments should I make? Although I had not set out to evaluate my curriculum or plan future lessons, I found myself planning next year's discussions, reflections, and activities that might highlight and clarify area and perimeter for my students.

REFLECTION

I soon had to report back to the group of teachers. I reminded myself that our original purposes in giving this assessment task to our students were (1) to evaluate the task and (2) to look for evidence of students' learning. Many of my students had no difficulty with the task, and their responses were impressive. I could select samples of what I felt was "quality work" to bring back to the group. But far more interesting to me were the issues around the work of those students who were confused by this task. Do I report back to the group that this was a good task? Was the difficulty experienced by some students caused by the task or by interference from the previous curriculum?

Why the Graph Breaks

My trigonometry class has seven juniors and thirteen seniors. My school uses a block schedule, and this year I am using some of the ninety-minute class period to have my students write in journals.

At some point in each class, I ask a question about something from the day's lesson. Then I give the students about ten minutes to respond in writing in their journals. I review their entries once a week and give the students up to 5 points for each entry. I use the following grading scale to determine how many points each student receives. There is no length requirement for answers to my questions; I look for quality rather than quantity.

JOURNAL GRADING SCALE

---

5 – Demonstrates full understanding. Explains with appropriate models.

4 – Shows basic understanding but does not go beyond minimal explanations.

3 – Has minor points missing or unclear.

2 – Shows gaps in concepts or understanding. Ideas are not well connected.

1 – Shows partial understanding. Arguments are incomplete.

0 – Shows little evidence of understanding.

My writing activity is met with opposition from some of my students almost daily. They ask, "Why do we have to write?" or they complain, "This is not English class!" Many students get frustrated trying to explain their thinking, and this frustration seems to affect their writing. A good example of this occurred last October.

Why the Graph Breaks

THE JOURNAL PROMPT

In a series of explorations, I asked students to use graphing calculators to graph the six trigonometric functions: $y = \sin(x)$, $y = \cos(x)$, $y = \sec(x)$, $y = \csc(x)$, $y = \tan(x)$, and $y = \cot(x)$. We had discussed that the sine and cosecant functions, the cosine and secant functions, and the tangent and cotangent functions were reciprocal functions. I asked students, working alone, to find the period and amplitude of each graph and to discover ways to transform the graphs through phase shifts, vertical shifts, and vertical stretching or shrinking. As a whole class, we talked about where to put asymptotes in the graphs of the secant, cosecant, tangent, and cotangent functions. This covered three class periods. The students did very well in their daily assignments. They were able to graph these functions using pencil and paper. They could answer my in-class questions about the graphs with little difficulty.

During the final day of exploration, we covered the graphs of the secant and cosecant functions. I then presented the following question to be answered in their journals:

> If sine and cosecant are reciprocal functions, explain why the graph of sine is continuous and the graph of cosecant is discontinuous.

There was the usual quiet moment as students read the question from the overhead screen. However, it quickly became clear to me, listening to murmurs and seeing furrowed brows and incredulous looks, that their frustration level was growing. Nathan got a few laughs when he mumbled, loud enough for me to hear, "This'll sure help my journal grade." It took a while before anyone began to write.

Why the Graph Breaks

A VARIETY OF RESPONSES

That evening I reviewed their journals to see how they responded to this question. Their responses fell into three distinct categories. Nathan's response was typical of the first type. Two other students had responses similar to his. (See **fig. 1.9**.)

FIG. 1.9

NATHAN'S RESPONSE

sine is opposite of cosecant and continuous is opposite of discontinuous

Stephanie and fourteen of her classmates fell into the second category of responses. They answered the question partially. (See **fig. 1.10** for Stephanie's response.)

FIG. 1.10

STEPHANIE'S RESPONSE

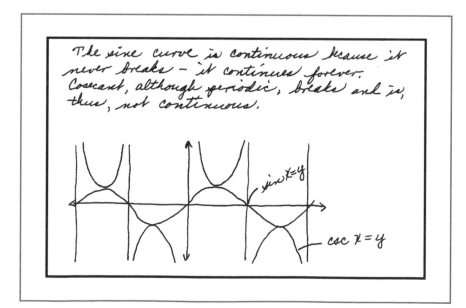

The sine curve is continuous because it never breaks – it continues forever. Cosecant, although periodic, breaks and is, thus, not continuous.

sin x = y

csc x = y

CHAPTER *1*

Why the Graph Breaks

Only two students explained why one graph was continuous and one was not. John was one of these students. (See **fig. 1.11** for John's response.)

FIG. 1.11

JOHN'S RESPONSE

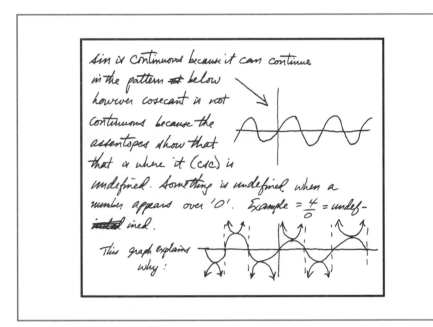

FRUSTRATION

As frustrated as my students seemed in class that day, it was frustrating for me to read these journal entries. From what I had observed in class, I expected higher-quality responses than I received. I wondered how well I had taught the concepts. Did the students just have a difficult time putting their thoughts down on paper, or did these journal entries reflect how much they really understood (or did not understand)? Was my question clear or confusing? Maybe they needed more guidance or additional prompts.

Writing in mathematics class is new for my students. Never before have they been asked to share their mathematical thinking in writing. I believe that all students should be able to do this, but I wonder: Will this get easier for them with time and practice? In the meantime, am I getting the best information I need to assess how much they know?

Peer Assessment and Self-Assessment

I teach geometry in a suburban high school where I have worked for twenty-eight years. I have participated in many in-service programs in mathematics education offered by my district and through local universities, and for the last few years I have immersed myself in a number of standards-based reforms. This year, I decided to ask my students in geometry class to assess themselves and each other on their homework.

Hoping to impress on my students that I value mathematical communication, I created the following holistic rubric. (See **fig. 1.12**.)

FIG. 1.12

HOLISTIC RUBRIC

PERFORMANCE STANDARDS FOR GEOMETRY HOMEWORK
NOTE: Grade will be reduced for all work turned in late.

	COMPLETENESS	ORGANIZATION	MATHEMATICAL COMMUNICATION	LEGIBILITY
A	■ Demonstrates an attempt to do every problem. Work is turned in on time.	■ Problems are easily located.	■ All necessary work to support a solution is shown.	■ Work can be easily deciphered. Diagrams are useful, neat, and orderly.
C	■ Demonstrates an attempt to do most problems.	■ Most problems are easily found.	■ There is evidence of a mathematical process, but solutions are incomplete.	■ Work can generally be deciphered. Diagrams are of some use.
F	■ Does few, if any, problems.	■ Problems are difficult to find.	■ May contain only answers or a very limited attempt to show a solution.	■ Work is difficult to read. It may contain scribbles, cross outs, and other distracting information.

Peer Assessment and Self-Assessment

SELF-ASSESSMENT

On the day the first homework assignment was due during the first week of school, I began geometry class by giving students a copy of the rubric. I asked them to read the rubric quietly. After two or three minutes, I told them to assign themselves a grade for their homework using the criteria in the rubric, to write that grade on a self-stick note, and to attach the note to their assignments. After a few minutes of puzzled looks and muffled conversation, I collected their assignments.

PEER ASSESSMENT

The next day, after recording scores and removing the self-stick notes, I put the students in groups and passed the assignments back, making sure students did not receive their own. I told them to use the rubric from the day before to grade the homework assignments given to each group.

Several awkward moments passed before my students began to talk among themselves. I walked around the classroom from group to group, listening to the conversations. The first group was struggling:

Grace:	Wow, this is much better than mine was! [*Looking around*] I wonder who has my paper …
Markeith:	[*Leaning over to Grace*] I can't read this. Is this a "six" or an "eight"?
Grace:	[*Pause*] I think it's a "six."
Linda:	[*Turning to me*] Why are we doing this? I don't know what grade it should get!

Calling for the attention of the whole class, I said, "As a group, read through the assignment first, and then see if one of the lines in the rubric describes what you read. Then decide on a grade, write it on the self-stick note, and attach it to the assignment."

That night, I recorded the scores from the peer assessments in my grade book alongside the scores students assigned in groups. Then I reviewed each assignment, writing on it the peer- and self-assigned scores, my own score, and some comments as feedback.

Peer Assessment and Self-Assessment

PROBLEMS WITH JOE

The next day, after I returned the students' assignments, I had a conversation with Joe. He and the peer group had given his assignment an A, but I had scored it a C.

> **Joe:** Why didn't you give me an A on my homework?
>
> **Teacher:** Tell me why you think it deserved an A.
>
> **Joe:** Well, I did all the problems, and I got the right answers.
>
> **Teacher:** That's true. But your paper isn't clear; I couldn't follow your explanation for the first problem, and you didn't say much at all in the second problem.
>
> **Joe:** So I get a C? I spent a lot of time on this, and I got all the right answers. Why isn't that enough?
>
> **Teacher:** In the rubric, it says you need to show all necessary work to support your answers in order to ...
>
> **Joe:** [*Interrupts angrily*] I *did* what was necessary. I showed my work and explained it. [*Walks away*] Never mind.

As Joe walked away, I wondered why he reacted so angrily. It bothered me that he and I did not seem to agree about what the rubric indicated. I was willing, however, to give him some time to use the rubric more. After seeing more students' work, maybe he would understand. There were not many disagreements between the students' scores and the ones I assigned; Joe was the only one who questioned my score.

SEVERAL MONTHS LATER

Several months have passed, and I still ask my students to do self-assessments and peer assessments regularly. At this point, more students complete more of their assignments. I am also convinced that having them read the work of others—and having them know their own work will be read by others—has improved the clarity and organization of the homework they submit. On occasion, students will give themselves a low grade.

I find myself, however, disagreeing more and more with their assessments. I had hoped to save some time by having students score homework themselves, but I am spending more time discussing discrepancies with them. Are students just giving themselves and their friends high grades? Are they taking the process seriously?

Early in the year, most students learned that they had to be neat, attempt all of the problems, and show their work. Since then, however, the quality of their work has not changed much. The grades they are assigning are creeping up. Most troubling is that I have had several other conversations like the one I had with Joe during the first week. What do I do now? How do I help students see that the quality of their work is important to me?

CHAPTER *1*

An Assessment Experiment

A few weeks ago, I walked into one of my mathematics classes to find the seniors in animated discussions. Their SAT scores had arrived in the mail, and they were all comparing results. Some of my best students were really disappointed. They did not do as well as they had hoped (or as well as I would have guessed, given their work in my class). I had noticed this before, but this time it really struck me! A lot of my students do not seem to perform as well on standardized tests as they do on similar types of questions in my class.

I knew I had not discovered anything new, but the stakes seemed higher for students in my state, where a passing grade on a statewide test is required each year for a student to get credit for a course. For this reason, I had been incorporating SAT and state test questions (or questions very similar to them) into my lessons and assessments regularly for some time. But there had to be more I could do besides using various item formats and sharing strategies for answering them. The disparity between performance in class and test scores still seemed to be there. I decided to do a little experiment with two of my freshman classes.

THE EXPERIMENT

It was still early in the year, and my classes were working on solving one-variable linear equations. I had already asked these students two types of standardized test questions:

1. Three times a number increased by 4 is 25. The number is:

   (a) 5   (b) 6   (c) 7   (d) 8   (e) 9

2. Package delivery companies charge according to the weight of the package. The Speedy Package Delivery Company charges 50 cents for the first ounce and 10 cents for each ounce after that. The Jiffy Company charges only 30 cents for the first ounce, but then charges 12 cents for each ounce after that. Which company would you use to ship a 12-ounce package?

   Answer: _____

An Assessment Experiment

Most of my ninth-graders found these questions easy and answered them correctly. I felt at the time that I got the assessment information I needed; most of them seemed able to solve simple linear sentences. At the same time I gave them practice with the two most common question formats used on standardized tests. What would happen, I wondered, if I asked these questions in different ways?

Last week, I asked the following questions on a quiz:

Solve and check: 1) $3x + 4 = 25$

2) $10x + 50 = 30 + 12x$

As I graded the quizzes, I took special note of how each student did on these two questions. Today, on another quiz, I asked the same students to solve these problems:

1. Sara bought several boxes of greeting cards from a catalog. Each box of cards cost $3, and she had to pay an additional $4 for shipping and handling on the entire order. If the entire bill was $25, how many boxes of cards did Sara buy?

2. The Acme Long-Distance Phone Company charges 50 cents for the first minute of a phone call and 10 cents for every minute after that. The World-Call Company charges only 30 cents for the first minute of a call but then charges 12 cents for each minute after that. What length call would cost the same if you use either company?

I just finished grading this most recent quiz. As a result of my experiment, I now have student responses to two questions, each of which I asked three different ways. The student responses seemed to depend on how I asked the questions.

An Assessment Experiment

THE RESULTS

For Question 1, almost every student answered the multiple-choice version of this question correctly. Almost as many answered the solve-the-equation version correctly. Because they showed what they did to get their answers, I observed that they used appropriate algebra steps. Surprisingly, even though about as many got the third, real-world-context version correct, most did so without even setting up an equation. They used a guess-and-check strategy to get the correct answer. (See **fig. 1.13** and **fig. 1.14**.)

FIG. 1.13

QUESTION 1, RESPONSE #1

> **Sara bought several boxes of greeting cards from a catalog. Each box of cards cost $3.00 and she had to pay an additional $4.00 for shipping and handling on the entire order. If the entire bill was $25.00, how many boxes of cards did Sara buy?**
>
> $$\begin{array}{r} 25 \\ -4 \\ \hline 21 \end{array}$$
> $3(7) = 21$ ⑦

FIG. 1.14

QUESTION 1, RESPONSE #2

> **Sara bought several boxes of greeting cards from a catalog. Each box of cards cost $3.00 and she had to pay an additional $4.00 for shipping and handling on the entire order. If the entire bill was $25.00, how many boxes of cards did Sara buy?**
>
> $3 \times 4 = 12 + 4 = 16$
> $3 \times 6 = 18 + 4 = 22$
> $3 \times 7 = 21 + 4 = 25$
> SO ⑦ BOXES

An Assessment Experiment

In Question 2, I was pleased when almost every student got the first "student-produced response" version correct. It is a word problem, after all, and this form usually causes trouble. Only about two-thirds of the students, however, solved the second version of this problem correctly. There are more algebra steps required to solve this equation, so I was not too surprised that more errors were made here. (See **fig. 1.15**.)

FIG. 1.15

A STUDENT'S ERROR

$$10x + 50 = 30 + 12x$$

$$\underline{-12x} \qquad \underline{-50}$$

$$-2x = 20$$

$$x = -10$$

I was surprised to see that fewer than one-third of my ninth graders were able to solve the last of the three versions of this question. Once again, almost no one even tried to set up an equation. The guess-and-check approach did not work very well in this problem. (See **fig. 1.16** and **fig. 1.17**.)

FIG. 1.16

QUESTION 2, RESPONSE #1

The Acme Long-Distance Phone Company charges 50 cents for the first minute of a phone call and 10 cents for every minute after that. The World-Call Company charges only 30 cents for the first minute of a call but then charges 12 cents for each minute after that. What length call would cost the same if you use either company?

$$10 \times 4 = 40 + 50 = 90$$
$$12 \times 4 = 48 + 30 = 78$$
$$10 \times 5 = 50 + 50 = 100$$
$$12 \times 5 = 60 + 30 = 90$$

$$10 \times 7 = 70 + 50 = 120$$
$$12 \times 7 = 82 + 30 = 112$$

Second company better

An Assessment Experiment

FIG. 1.17

QUESTION 2, RESPONSE #2

> The Acme Long-Distance Phone Company charges 50 cents for the first minute of a phone call and 10 cents for every minute after that. The World-Call Company charges only 30 cents for the first minute of a call but then charges 12 cents for each minute after that. What length call would cost the same if you use either company?
>
> 50, 60, 70, 80, 90, 100, 110, 120
>
> 30, 42, 54, 66, 78, 90   90¢

My experiment confirmed for me that when you ask the same question in different forms, it affects students' answers. What is it about the ways I asked each question? Were the different forms simply unfamiliar, or did they ask different things from students?

Some unexpected things came from my experiment. For example, almost no one recognized that I asked the same questions over and over, and very few students used algebra to solve the problems unless the equation was already given.

The conclusions I drew after the first round of questions about what my students understood seem a little naive now. But after all three rounds of questions, I have a much better sense of what each student understands about this topic.

My students have to practice with questions like the ones they will see on the state test and the SAT. They need to be able to see past the form of the question to the important mathematical questions being asked. These tests are just too important. But if I want to learn whether my students can solve problems, I have to ask them questions they haven't practiced. I have a full curriculum to cover. My experiment showed me that standardized test questions only give me some information about what the students actually know. I need to use a variety of question forms to build a full picture of my students' strengths and weaknesses. Where's the balance?

Chapter 2

Cases about Scoring Assessment

Right or Wrong

Recently, a colleague and I were asked to lead a workshop on assessment strategies for in-service elementary and middle school teachers. The main goal of the workshop was to have teachers examine their own assessment practices, debate the importance of consistency in grading, and recognize the usefulness in developing scoring schemes.

A TASK WITH STUDENTS' WORK

The problem below was taken from a sixth-grade mathematics problem-solving book (Charles, Mason, and Gardner 1985). We presented it to the teachers, along with the actual work of two students attempting to solve it. (See **fig. 2.1** and **fig. 2.2**.)

Kennedy collected 225 tape cassettes and 4 old shoe boxes to put them in. If he puts the same number of cassettes in each box, how many extra cassettes will there be?

FIG. 2.1

CHRIS'S WORK

FIG. 2.2

PAT'S WORK

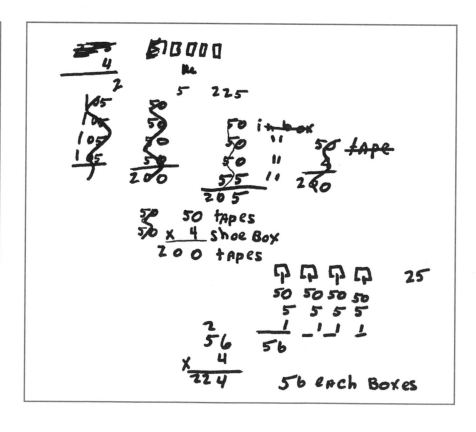

Right or Wrong

TEACHER ASSIGNMENT

We asked the teachers to score each of the work samples, giving each a score from 0 to 5. We wanted them to score these samples using their own criteria. Hence, no scoring scheme was given. We also asked the teachers to provide rationales for their scores.

DISCUSSION OF CHRIS'S WORK

We first focused the discussion on Chris's work. Teachers reported their scores on a tally sheet. The scores ranged from 0 to 4 with a mean of about 1.5. Below is a table showing the number of teachers assigning each of the five possible scores:

The Distribution of Scores of Sixteen Teachers Assessing Chris's Work						
Scores	5	4	3	2	1	0
Number of responses	0	1	2	4	6	3

The discussion began with several teachers debating whether Chris actually understood the problem.

Frank: I think Chris knew what to do and that it was division. So, I gave 4 points.

Ravelle: No way! This student did not have a clue which operation he was supposed to be using. But I gave him 1 point for effort.

Leah: No, look again. See the order in which Chris did the operations. I think he figured out that addition and multiplication were wrong. Then he settled on division. So I gave him 3 points.

Frances: How can you assume that? I don't think he deserves any points because I don't think he understands what is going on in the problem. But I gave him a grade of 1 for trying.

Paula: I agree with you for wanting to give Chris some points for effort. With my classes I am pleased when my students show effort. I want to reward them for trying. Shouldn't he get more points than a student who doesn't even attempt to solve it?

Leah: And he showed the ability to add and multiply and is beginning to learn division. I still think he should get 3 points.

Ruby: I gave Chris 2 points. Chris knows addition, half a point, knows how to multiply, 1 point, and knows how to divide but forgot the decimal, half a point.

Lois: Chris did not identify the answer, minus 1.

Sandi: So, where's the answer? I can't give any points for this.

Right or Wrong

DISCUSSION OF PAT'S WORK

After everyone had shared his or her ideas about Chris's work, we asked the teachers to report their scores for Pat's work. The range of scores was the same, from 0 to 4, but the mean of about 3 was much higher than the mean for Chris's work.

Scores	5	4	3	2	1	0
The Distribution of Scores of Sixteen Teachers Assessing Pat's Work						
Number of responses	0	9	4	0	1	2

Katherine:	He knew a strategy for getting the answer, so I gave him 4 points.
Frances:	I also gave 4 points because he logically pursued part of the problem using pictures and estimation.
Ravelle:	Yes, the use of pictures shows he has understanding of the problem.
Ruby:	I withheld a point because Pat had difficulty using the algorithm to help him with division.
Walt:	A sixth grader should know how to divide. I took off 2 points.
Frances:	He understood conceptually the idea of division. He just didn't use the algorithm. I think he solved it creatively.
Lois:	I took off 1 point because he did not tell how many extra cassettes there were. He didn't answer the question either.
Sandi:	I cannot give any points. A math problem is either right or wrong. He didn't solve it. Chris didn't either.
Rebecca:	I agree with Sandi. If these two students were on the job, their answers would be worthless. What if Pat was building a bridge and made incorrect calculations. People could get hurt!
Paula:	This is crazy! These students were in school, and not on a job and should not be judged as workers. They should be given points for their thinking.
Frank:	This problem is about cassettes, not bridges, and nobody is going to get hurt! Pat showed some understanding of the problem and deserves some credit.

Right or Wrong

SCORING ISSUES

After all had expressed their reasons for their scores, the focus of the discussion changed. The conversation moved away from the specific work of these two students to a more general discussion about scoring. Should they be evaluating computation or understanding? How can you give points for both? Aren't both important?

> **Frances:** If you wanted to assess a student's ability to divide, you could give him a straight division problem. Wasn't it more important to check for understanding?

> **Ravelle:** If we are checking for understanding, we need more information about how the student really thought about it.

> **Paula:** Yes, you really need multiple methods of assessment.

Some teachers thought so strongly about some issues that they restated their beliefs. Some thought that students should get credit for trying. Others were still adamant that no points should be given when the answer is incorrect. Then someone said that in advanced mathematics, mathematicians could work for a long time without getting an answer. But the process is still important. Answers are not everything.

Our time was almost up, but the teachers were very engaged. I asked them if the fact that they had used different criteria to score the work was a problem. We began to discuss the issue of consistency in grading. How subjective had the scores been? Should we try to make grading as objective as possible?

After a short break, the teachers returned to discuss the usefulness of developing a rubric. Would it be possible for these teachers to reach a consensus on what a quality response would look like? Could a rubric capture the different aspects of the problem-solving process that they valued—understanding, computation, effort, and correct answer? Would a rubric improve the consistency in grading?

A Difference of Opinion

"Can students score other students' work?" I asked myself once again, staring down at the updated list of the Unit Assessment Tasks in our new assessment package. I still like the idea of having students look critically at other students' work, but according to the trial run we made last spring, this seems to be a troublesome process.

BACKGROUND

My district was in the second year of a new pilot mathematics curriculum. All teachers in grades 6 through 8 in our district had implemented it as a new program. In the fall, I was part of a group of mathematics teachers who began working on assessment tools for the curriculum. Through the development of a cohesive collection of assessment tasks, we hoped to establish some common ground that would then promote future discussion on students' learning and mathematical understanding throughout the district.

In creating the assessment tools, we began by choosing assessment tasks for many of the units used in the series. After selecting a task and trying it ourselves, we developed scoring rubrics that described the criteria necessary for each score listed on the rubric. We gave the tasks to pilot teachers to administer to their eighth-grade students. Then, using this student work, we selected anchor papers. These papers were chosen as examples that accurately reflected each rubric level, and as such, they were to be used as scoring guides. We planned to distribute the task, rubric, and anchor papers to all middle school mathematics teachers in the district to be incorporated into the curriculum.

STUDENTS AS ASSESSORS

Looking to improve students' achievement on open-ended questions, we also wanted students to have the experience of scoring their classmates' papers. Our hypothesis was that this scoring experience would give students a better idea of what was expected of them when responding to open-ended questions.

As part of the pilot team, I administered an assessment task to my eighth-grade class. The task, which examined the relationship between volume and surface area, concluded about three weeks of work on the topic. (See **fig. 2.3** for task and **fig. 2.4** for rubric.)

FIG. 2.3

RECTANGULAR SOLIDS TASK

RECTANGULAR SOLIDS

Given a rectangular solid with volume 24 cubic centimeters:

1. Draw and label dimensions for as many different rectangular solids as possible with a volume of 24 cubic centimeters.

2. Find the volume and surface area for each solid.

3. After you have completed parts 1 and 2 above, describe the rectangular solids that have the largest and smallest surface areas.

A Difference of Opinion

FIG. 2.4

RECTANGULAR SOLIDS RUBRIC

LEVEL	PERFORMANCE
4 + **Exemplary**	■ Goes beyond the expectations of a "4," with additional insights, recognition of patterns, and applications ■ Recognizes the existence of prisms whose dimensions are not expressed in integers ("Nonintegral" dimensions*) ■ Identifies a cube with edges approximately 2.9 cm in length as the rectangular prism with the minimum surface area
4 **Well Done**	■ Addresses all sections of the problem ■ Draws and labels all six rectangular prisms with "integral" dimensions and conveys their three-dimensional shape ■ Correctly computes surface area for all rectangles ■ Describes clearly and accurately the dimensions of the prisms with the largest and the smallest surface area
3 **Some Revision Needed**	■ Addresses all sections of the problem ■ Draws and labels three or more rectangular prisms with integral dimensions and conveys their three-dimensional shape ■ Correctly computes surface area for at least three prisms ■ Describes clearly and accurately the dimensions of the prisms with the largest and the smallest surface area
2 **Extensive Revision Needed**	■ Addresses the problem ■ Draws and labels at least two different rectangular prisms with integral dimensions ■ Attempts surface area computation ■ Attempts written description of prisms that is relevant but not necessarily clear or accurate. ■ Demonstrates understanding of concept of surface area as distinct from volume
1 **Restart (More Instruction Needed)**	■ Addresses the problem ■ Shows little or no understanding of either volume or surface area ■ Shows little or no computation to support conclusions
0	■ Makes no attempt; paper is blank or contains unintelligible marks ■ Writes "I don't understand" or equivalent

A Difference of Opinion

To test the scoring tool, I, along with a couple of other pilot teachers, planned to run a trial of the student-scoring process a few days later. In the trial, we gave our students the seven anchor papers with the teachers' scores removed to score according to the rubric. If they understood the problem and the rubric, then their scores should match the teachers' scores. Afterward, the students would continue to score work that had not yet been scored.

THE TRIAL RUN

On the day of the trial, Eric and Maureen, my two companion teachers, arrived at the door in time for my third-period mathematics class. Calling the attention of my students who were checking homework answers, I introduced Eric and Maureen as teachers who have come to help me with a new assessment. Informing the class that I would need their help as well, I divided the students into groups of four.

Eric passed out a set of anchor papers and a rubric to each group. I quickly went over the content of the rubric, explaining that the number in the left column represented the score for the description on the right. I was confident that everyone understood the format of the rubric, since I had used rubrics in class before.

"Now, I'd like each group to score the papers using the rubric," I said as I continued to explain the activity. "As a group, you must decide on one score for each paper."

My classes often worked in groups, so I knew they understood what arriving at a single score meant. Eric, Maureen, and I wandered around the room as the groups examined the anchor papers and determined a score. When everyone had finished, the students began reporting the scores group by group.

The students' scores agreed with the teachers' scores in all instances except one—the anchor paper that teachers believed reflected a perfect 2. The groups of students unanimously considered it a 3. (See **fig. 2.5**.)

A Difference of Opinion

FIG. 2.5

ANCHOR PAPER FOR A 2

8th Grade Final Assessment

Glencoe. Unit 14, "Run for Cover"

Rectangular Solids

Given a rectangular solid with a volume of 24 cm³:

measurment (l,w,H)

1) Draw and label <u>dimensions</u> for as many different rectangular solids as possible with a volume of 24 cm³:

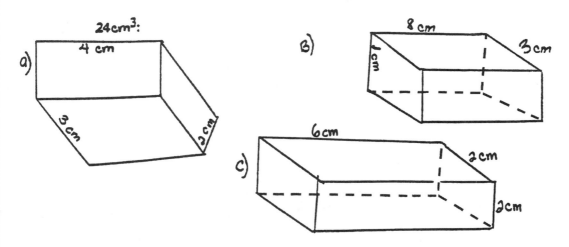

24cm³:

a) 4 cm, 3 cm, 2 cm

B) 8 cm, 3cm, 1cm

c) 6cm, 2cm, 2cm

2) Find the volume and surface area for each solid:

a) volume: 4×3×2 = 24 cm³
   surface area: 4+3+2 = 9 cm³

B) volume: 8×3×1 = 24 cm³
   surface area: 8+3+1 = 12 cm³

c) volume: 6×2×2 = 2A cm³
   surface area: 6+2+2 = 10 cm³

3) After you have completed parts 1 and 2 above, describe the rectangular solids which have the largest and smallest surface area.

FIGURE a HAVE THE smallest surface area WITH THE LENGTH EQUAL TO 4, WIDT EQUAL TO 2 OND HEIGHT EQUAL TO 3. ALL OF THOSE cm. NUMBER EQUAL TO 9 cm, AND OUT OF ALL MY FIGURE IT GOT THE smallest surface area.

A Difference of Opinion

Although taken aback, I decided to conduct a class discussion. I realized that we needed to resolve the discrepancy before allowing the students to continue scoring. Maureen, Eric, and I listened while students presented arguments to support their score of a 3, hoping we would uncover the cause of the disagreement. My students started by remarking on the presentation of the paper.

"The paper is neat," commented Kerry, a conscientious and attentive student.

"They made nice drawings," noted Youseff. Judging by the nodding heads of the other students, everyone liked the drawings.

"Okay, now I'd like you to consider only the surface area computation and the other parts of the rubric that show mathematical knowledge and thinking," I said, trying to elicit comments from the class that reflected their understanding of the mathematics.

"The student calculated the volume and surface area for each figure, but didn't finish the problem."

"The student picked the right figure for the smallest surface area."

Despite an array of responses, no one commented that the math was done incorrectly! Recognizing, too, that these students did not see any mistakes in the work, Maureen motioned to me from across the room with a look of disbelief. It was clear that they did not have a strong understanding of the concept of surface area.

The students wondered if their scores were the same as ours. We showed them our scores and pointed out why we gave this paper a 2. No one seemed impressed. The students did change their scores, although probably not because they understood their error of judgment, but because "the teachers must be right." We finished the period—without allowing any further scoring by the students.

Later that afternoon, as I organized the papers spread out on my desk and prepared to go home, my thoughts drifted to the student-scoring experiment. I wondered how appropriate it is for students to score other students' papers if they do not have a clear idea of the mathematical concepts involved. Was the scoring process a valuable learning experience for the students doing the scoring? After our explanation of the errors, could these students score the rest of the papers reliably and consistently? Would I be assured that every student who submits a paper would get a fair and sensible evaluation? As I shut the classroom door behind me, my thoughts continued to drift: what could we do to make the student scoring more successful?

On the Other Side of the Desk

While preparing my Discrete Mathematics final exam, I wondered how best to assess the progress of my students. My major concern was to conclude the grading period on a positive note, so I offered the class this alternative:

"Would you like to take a two-hour written exam, ... or teach a lesson to your peers for fifteen to eighteen minutes?"

What a choice for my class to make! I was pleasantly surprised that they all accepted the challenge and opted for the teaching.

Currently, all students in our high school are required to take three years of mathematics. Those planning a career in science or mathematics complete the traditional four-year course sequence of algebra, geometry, precalculus, and calculus. Our department decided to offer a brand-new course, Discrete Mathematics. It was developed as an option for an anticipated fourth math course graduation requirement. It not only provided students with an alternative to the traditional mathematics sequence, but it might also spark the students' interest in new areas of mathematics.

"How are you going to grade us?" asked Tina, one of the four juniors in a class of twenty seniors.

"Can we do it with partners?" questioned Ramo. Lacking confidence in math, Ramo is always looking for ways to improve his grade.

"What are we supposed to teach?" inquired Svan, probably the first time that a subject had attracted his attention.

In response to this barrage of questions, I prepared a guideline, giving much thought to the evaluation process. (See **fig. 2.6**.)

On the Other Side of the Desk

FIG. 2.6

DISCRETE MATHEMATICS FINAL EXAM GUIDELINE

DISCRETE MATHEMATICS
Final Exam

Objective: A team of two students will *study*, *research*, and *teach* their classmates a lesson for their midterm examination. The topic can be picked from, but is not limited to, Excursions in Modern Mathematics.

Topics from Excursions in Modern Mathematics: Any topic not covered in this semester. You may choose other topics from sources such as the library, Internet, etc.

Time limit in teaching: 15 to 18 minutes. (Points will be deducted if it is more than 18 or less than 15 minutes.)

Preparation and support: Approval of topic by Friday, Dec. 20. A brief lesson plan is due after the holiday. Some class periods in January will be set aside for refining the teaching technique and practice.

Rubrics of the teaching will be distributed.

Method of teaching is up to you. You may use the chalkboard, overhead projector, videotape, TV clips, graphing calculator, or computer programs. This is the time for you to shine.

Alternative Final Exam: A two-hour sit-down written test of all the topics we have done this semester on Thursday, Jan. 20.

Please let me know **before Friday, Jan. 10**, if you so choose.

Evaluation: The class will participate in evaluation. Each student will grade the teaching according to the guideline from the rubrics. Each student will also earn points toward his or her own final exam grade for doing so. Written reaction to the teaching will be evaluated. However, points will be deducted for disrupting or interfering with the teaching. Please remember to treat your fellow students with courtesy and respect as you would expect them to treat you.

Guests: Faculty, administrator, or parent evaluation is welcome.

Grade: This final exam teaching will be counted as 1/3 of the semester grade. The grade is composed of

>> Peer evaluation: 15 percent
>>
>> Presenter's self-evaluation: 5 percent
>>
>> Guest evaluation: 10 percent
>>
>> Teacher evaluation: 70 percent or 80 percent (including 5 percent for evaluating other students' presentations)

Exam Schedule: Starting **Friday, Jan. 10**, two teams will teach each day. Time assignment will be done through lottery. You may, however, switch with another team before Monday, Jan. 6, if both parties agree to do so.

Exam period on Jan. 20 will be reserved for makeups and end-of-the-semester, student-teacher conferences.

On the Other Side of the Desk

Throughout my twenty-eight years of teaching, Fairness to Each Other has been my motto. I was concerned that some students might react negatively or disrespectfully to the presenters. This prompted me to formulate the peer evaluation grading component. This component, on completion, allotted 5 percent to the evaluator's grade and counted 15 percent of the presenter's grade. Our high school takes pride in its student population and in the fact that more than 90 percent of its 1300 students go to college. It also welcomes community involvement, so I decided to invite parents as guest evaluators. I wanted to make sure the students took the project seriously and put forth their best effort.

CHOOSING PARTNERS

In class, the students formed their own teams of two by selecting their own partners. They had done group work before, so forming teams was not too much of a problem.

"I don't have a partner. What shall I do?" asked Svan. Svan tends to sleep a lot during class, claiming he has to work long hours to support his car. "Pema does not have a partner either. Do you want to work with her?" I asked. "No, not really. Can I ..." Svan paused, not sure if it were permissible, "can I work with my brother? He just came back from college for the winter break." "I don't see that as a problem, if he agrees." I figured Svan could use the help.

GETTING TO WORK

Tina: What are you doing? [*To the teacher, who was putting a transparency on the overhead projector*]

Teacher: We are going to ...

Tina: Not a new lesson!

Teacher: Uh huh.

Tina: What about the exam that we are supposed to work on?

Teacher: What do you mean? Aren't you going to work on it together after school?

Ramo: After school? I have basketball practice.

Vinny: I have a track meet.

Svan: I have real work after school. We don't have time to get together to work on your exam. Can we do it in class?

Understanding their complaints, I decided to let the students use class time for their teaching project. "All right. Get together with your partner. Find two topics in your book to work on."

As students found their partners, I passed Ramo's team. "What are you guys doing? Are you working on these sneakers as your project?" I asked. Ramo, a varsity basketball player, was checking out a sneaker catalog with his partner. "No, we are not. We will put it away in a minute," Ramo replied, his eyes still on the page. "You may do a statistics topic on the sneaker prices, you know," I suggested halfheartedly and continued to check on the other teams.

On the Other Side of the Desk

"How about you, Danny? Why are you working on your college application? Isn't it a little late?" I asked. I frowned to myself and looked over at Tonya. "What's that, Tonya? Prom dresses ... and what else? You guys are supposed to be working on your projects." I raised my voice, annoyed that almost everyone was doing something other than the teaching project. "Don't worry, we have plenty of time to get it done!"

The next day, hoping to motivate the class, I decided to let students pick the topics on a first-come, first-served basis. The competition to pick the easiest topic from the textbook quickly got the teams busy and involved. It was the beginning of the students' commitment to my experiment. Also, to help the students focus on the task, I devised an outline of a lesson plan for the following period. (See **fig. 2.7**.) I asked each team to fill it out and turn it in by the end of the period.

FIG. 2.7

DISCRETE MATHEMATICS LESSON PLAN

LESSON PLAN   Team Members:_____
                                                              _____

DISCRETE MATHEMATICS
Final Exam

Title:_____

Source:_____ (Include page numbers)

Props. posters. etc.:_____(Can you make them razzle-dazzle?)

_____

Electronic equipment used:_____ (Need a VCR, overhead projector?)

_____

Preliminary preparation prior to presentation: _____

_____

Presentation strategy:_____

_____

_____

_____

Methods of involving the class:_____

_____

_____

_____

Our clincher will be_____ (That is how you ace this exam!)

_____

_____

CHAPTER 2

On the Other Side of the Desk

CHANGE OF MIND

Nana: Can I take the written exam?

Teacher: How come?

Nana: I changed my mind.

Teacher: Is there any reason for that?

Nana: We … we couldn't find a topic we liked.

Teacher: Anything else?

Nana: Well, we never really spoke in front of the class before. Not for that long a period anyway.

Teacher: Tell you the truth, Nana, I would like not having to make up a two-hour exam just for two of you. Besides …

Nana: Besides what?

Teacher: Don't you hate written tests? Remember last year in my Precalculus Honors class? You were in tears after you got your second test back. [*I thought about Nana's test performance last year (and her tears). I wanted her to conclude the Discrete Mathematics course with more confidence.*]

Nana: That's only because I didn't know how to take your tests. I used to do very well in other math classes.

Teacher: What was the difference?

Nana: I don't know. But I do know I forget just about everything after the exam.

Teacher: So why ask for a written exam? Just for a grade? Tell you what, Nana. If I tell you that there is no way you will fail this presentation, will you give it a try?

Nana: Well, it is not the grade that I am concerned about. It is … I don't know.

Teacher: Let me put it this way, Nana, you are going to college in a few months, right? Do you realize that you will have to make a lot of decisions by yourself? I understand that it is easier for you to take the written exam. That's what you are used to doing.

Nana came from the Philippines many years ago, and I am from China, so I knew that her early education had been similar to mine.

Teacher: This project you are going to present will be entirely your choice. You call the shots. You make the decisions. I want you to take advantage of this opportunity to show yourself how independent you can be. Why don't you talk it over with your partner tonight? Find a topic you both like. Let me know tomorrow. Maybe I can give you some help. How's that?

Nana listened without saying a word and eventually nodded her head. She would try.

On the Other Side of the Desk

LAYING THE GROUNDWORK

The date of each team's presentation was determined by lottery. The students completed all the preliminary work before winter break. After the break, six days remained before the start of the presentations. I handed out the rubric to be used for evaluating the presentations. (See **fig. 2.8**.)

FIG. 2.8

DISCRETE MATHEMATICS RUBRIC

DISCRETE MATHEMATICS
Final Exam

RUBRIC

Team Members: _____   Evaluator: _____
_____   Date: _____

	CONTENT	DELIVERY	CREATIVITY	Q & A
5	■ No errors ■ Well understood	■ Clear ■ Concise ■ Logical ■ Thorough	■ Innovative ■ Lots of effort	■ Questions encouraged and answered effectively
3	■ Minor errors ■ Fairly well understood	■ Not quite clear ■ Logical ■ Adequate ■ Read occasionally	■ Routine ■ Adequate effort	■ Questions answered satisfactorily ■ Admit not knowing answer
1	■ Some major errors ■ Hardly understood	■ Confusing ■ Illogical ■ Incomplete ■ Read from notes	■ Lacking effort	■ Most questions not answered satisfactorily ■ Failed to admit not knowing answer

Score:

Please comment on the lesson taught. Use the back of the page for more space.

1. What was the best part of the lesson?

_____

_____

2. Any ideas or helpful hints on how the lesson could be improved or clarified? Be specific.

_____

_____

On the Other Side of the Desk

Students were surprised by the expectations laid out in the rubric. Many modified their lessons when they noticed creativity as one of the categories in the rubric. To help them further, I suggested a rehearsal in front of the class, but I was amazed to find that none of the teams wanted to do this. They were afraid their creative ideas might be copied!

Teacher: Svan, how is your project coming along?

Svan: It will be good. My brother cannot come for the presentation. He has to do something on that day.

Teacher: Oh. Do you need him at all?

Svan: No, I don't think so. I will videotape the lesson. Can I?

Svan's request to videotape his lesson prompted me to wonder about the possibility of videotaping all presentations. Would students perform better knowing that their presentations were being recorded? When I asked the class the next day about videotaping their presentations, no one objected. In fact, a student taking a course in video production volunteered to do it for us.

To further ensure a successful and memorable six days of students as teachers, I invited three parents, a few teachers, one counselor, and two principals to act as guest evaluators.

THE BIG DAY

The long-awaited "exam" finally arrived on a Friday. Eager to find out how the experiment would unfold, I went to school a little earlier than usual. Everyone showed up on time. I handed out the rubric and reminded everybody to rate the teaching presentations with written comments. With the camera ready to roll, I signaled Ramo and his partner to start. From a piece of paper that he had shown me several days ago, Ramo copied college graduates' salaries onto the board. The topic they picked was "Graphing and Summarizing Data: A Graphical Representation."

On the Other Side of the Desk

The room was quiet and orderly, and everyone waited patiently for the presenters to finish. I was stunned by the tranquil atmosphere. It was a totally different class! After Ramo carefully drew a bar graph on the board, time ran out. I gave them two more minutes to finish the lesson. As they rushed to conclude, Ramo quickly placed a transparency of Highest Basketball Field Goal Percentages on the overhead projector as an additional example. The presentation was less than I expected. One comment from a student evaluator said, "They faced more time to the board than the audience." While the audience completed their rubrics, I asked the presenters to fill out a self-evaluation form. (See **fig. 2.9**.)

Ramo and his partner graded the presentation an A.

FIG. 2.9

SELF-EVALUATION FORM

SELF-EVALUATION

To be completed after the presentation. Each member must respond.

How successful was your teaching? Did you accomplish what you planned?

_____

_____

_____

Would you do it again? Or would you teach it differently?

_____

_____

_____

What grade would you give to yourself? Why?

_____

_____

_____

PROJECT EVALUATION

Please give your evaluation of the overall project. What do you think you learned from this experience?

_____

_____

_____

_____

_____

CHAPTER 2

On the Other Side of the Desk

The second presentation used colorful posters to illustrate the essential points of the topic, "Apportionment." A transparency showed the rules of the Hamilton Method as each partner took turns explaining the method. Their voices were loud and clear, and they helped each other in responding to questions from the class. Then, using 150 pieces of Jolly Rancher candies as the available congressional seats, they instructed the class to apportion them according to the Hamilton Method. They awarded correct answers with a candy, and the remaining candies were distributed to the rest of the class to wrap up the presentation. This was the quality of presentation that I hoped the students might achieve. They gave a much more dynamic and sophisticated lesson than Ramo's bar graph.

To conclude the period, I asked the class to reflect on the two presentations during the weekend and urged them to refine their presentations for the following week.

Over the next five days, the rest of the pairs made their presentations.

EVALUATING THE EXPERIMENT

A few days after the last presentation, I brought doughnuts and soft drinks to class, and I asked the students to fill out a project evaluation form. (See **fig. 2.10**.)

FIG. 2.10

DISCRETE MATHEMATICS REFLECTION: A POSTEVALUATION

DISCRETE MATHEMATICS
REFLECTION: A POSTEVALUATION

Please comment on your final exam experience. Be candid.

_____

_____

_____

_____

Please comment on the Discrete Mathethmatics course you had this semester.

_____

_____

_____

_____

Would you recommend this course to your friend? Why or why not?

_____

_____

_____

_____

On the Other Side of the Desk

I assured everyone that the grades were already done and that as soon as the forms were turned in, they would receive their grade. Ramo insisted on seeing his grade first before filling out the evaluation form. I did not want to make a big deal out of it, so I let him look at his grade. "How come I get only a B? I don't think it's fair," complained Ramo.

Ramo would like to get high grades, but usually he has never gotten anything higher than a C. We have had several discussions about his grades in the past, and his point of contention has always been that he was not being graded fairly.

"Well, Ramo, let's see how your grade was calculated." I took out his peer and guest evaluations. I leafed through the stack slowly, showing him that quite a few 3s and 4s were given from a scale of 1 to 5. His was one of three teams that had gotten such a low rating.

"Ramo, your own comprehension of the topic was fine, but you know this was not merely a presentation of what you had learned about the subject. You were supposed to make us understand what you had learned. Simply writing a table of figures and drawing the bar graph in front of us was not enough for an A. Besides, I told you I was willing to make a copy of these figures on the transparency for the overhead projector to save valuable time. You never came back to me. I suggested to you also that you should find a variety of examples to get the class involved in the process. I didn't see it happen in your presentation." I was not sure if Ramo was convinced that he was being treated fairly, but he left without further protest.

BACK BEHIND THE DESK

What was the outcome of all these preparations? Was it worth the risk? Would I do it again? In a review of the quotes taken from student evaluations, the answer presents itself:

> I am glad that an official test wasn't given. Many students don't do as well on tests, including myself....

> It was fun. I had a great time making the video. Also the concepts that I learned stayed with me better because I had to put all the facts to memory.

> Most of the groups tried to explain it in our terms. The use of Visual Aids also helped to cement our understanding.

> It gave me a chance to use my creativity. I think it influenced students to learn in a different way.

> It [the teaching presentation] shows if a student really understands the subject.

> Teaching is very difficult. And that trying to interest the class about a dry topic is very difficult.

> I learned what we were capable of doing. I learned a lot, beginning with learning how to teach a class, learning the actual material, and learning to respect other students as well as the teacher.

> It was good to be on the other side of the desk for once.

CHAPTER *2*

The Enormous Gulp

As part of our study of calculus each year, I assign the Can Project to my students. Following our study of optimization, the project requires students to build a 12-ounce cylindrical soda can that uses a minimum amount of aluminum (or in our case, cardboard). A second part of the project requires students to write a letter to the soda company of their choice asking why soda cans use more aluminum than is absolutely necessary. (In some classes, these letters were actually sent, and replies were received.) To grade these projects, I created a scoring rubric based on the following criteria:

■ The can's height should equal the diameter.

■ The letters to the soda companies needed to be literate and make a well-reasoned mathematical argument.

REVISING THE TASK

In September 1994, *Scientific American* ran an article on can design entitled "The Aluminum Beverage Can." The article gave a thorough explanation of how the design of aluminum cans has evolved. In particular, it noted that the aluminum used in the top and bottom of the cans is significantly thicker than the aluminum on the sides. The original project asking students to minimize materials to make the cans certainly did not take this into account.

This year, I decided to see what my students would come up with if they read the *Scientific American* article. I gave them the following assignment:

THE GREAT CAN PROJECT

Congratulations! You have just been hired by the Stellar Soda Company to design a soda can for its new product, the Enormous Gulp. You were hired because of your extensive knowledge of calculus and your willingness to do the necessary research to protect our environment (and production costs) by using a minimum amount of aluminum.

The assignment: You are to build a soda can that will hold exactly 15 ounces of soda and use a minimum amount of aluminum. Your can should be accompanied by a report to the president of the company explaining how and why you used the design with calculations to prove to her that your math did create a can that holds 15 ounces and uses a minimum amount of aluminum. Can and report are due in the president's hands no later than Monday, 13 February. Late projects may jeopardize your job rating. Poor design may cause you to be canned. Please note that the president is able to follow only a clear, reasoned mathematical argument.

The Enormous Gulp

GRADING THE DESIGN

I did not know what to expect from the Enormous Gulp, and therefore I was unsure how I would grade the projects. The door was now open to more than one possible design because I was not sure how my students would account for the greater thickness of the top and bottom of the can. Several possible solutions came to mind. They might do any of the following:

■ Calculate the ratio of the diameter to height of a 12-ounce can and extrapolate for the 15-ounce can

■ Use the fact that the top and bottom are approximately three times as thick as the sides, and some calculus, to design the can

■ Ignore the *Scientific American* article and design a "square" can

■ Use a marketing ploy and ignore the materials usage question entirely

As a teacher of Advanced Placement calculus, I've spent many hours looking at old AP questions and the scoring rubrics that accompany them. Free-response questions are worth 9 points; each point is carefully spelled out. Part of my job is to train my students to craft a response that not only is correct but also has the necessary components to earn a high score. When I encountered students' resistance about whether a specific component is necessary, it was easy for me to wave my hands and deny responsibility for the grading because it was not of my doing. In using such rubrics, I find that there is something comforting for me, the teacher, to be told exactly how to award each point, as though I am somehow freed from the responsibility of deciding what standards to impose on my students.

In contrast to the AP questions, the Enormous Gulp project was much more open-ended. I wondered if it would be sufficient to look for good mathematics and a mathematical argument that is consistent with the data or that states which solutions would be best. Is it fair to my students to decide these issues after I see the projects, or does that diminish objectivity? In general, I was able to say that a reasonable can coupled with a cogent, thoughtful argument was their goal. I was not sure where we were headed, but I was open to the possibility that even the most thoughtful students might not be able to do the necessary calculations to produce an optimal product.

DISPLAYING THE DESIGN

With projects turned in, it was easy to see where we were—twenty four cardboard, clay, or Styrofoam soda cans displayed on a table gave an instant visual report of what the students did. Most of the cans were "square," their height equal to their diameter. A few cans were clearly different and presented the first insight into what the students understood and were capable of producing. Checking the accompanying written reports also helped me understand what my students had done.

The Enormous Gulp

Most students did a classic optimization problem producing a can that minimized surface area. Their arguments did not even address the question of minimizing aluminum. In most cases, it was impossible to know whether this was because they had not done the requisite research, whether they had not understood the assignment or the *Scientific American* article that talked about can design, or whether they could not do the mathematics. One student did say, "My can does not follow any of the guidelines mentioned in the *Scientific American* article. This is because I had no idea how to create a can that resembled the one described in the article."

A student with more bravado simply said, "My design is simple. It's minimized. It's aluminized!" The square can projects became the standard for a respectable, but not outstanding, grade.

Two students who created square cans included written arguments that they had "wanted to do a sphere but found the smallest surface area to be a cylinder." The calculations in their reports were wrong. It was easy to penalize them for this error, although I recognized that they might well have been on the right track logically. The fact that they had more than two weeks to complete their projects meant to me that they should have checked and double-checked their work.

The more interesting projects earned the highest grades. One student created a square can but included the following disclaimer, reflecting her understanding of the challenge, if not her ability to rise to it:

> **Note:** As was written in my assignment, I was hired to design this can because of my expertise in Calculus, and my job was to find the can with the smallest surface area, which I have done. May I suggest that you have a talk with some scientists about structural integrity, and whether or not this is a feasible design for holding a soda can. You might also want to discuss this design with the advertising department before making any decisions because the shape does in fact make the can appear smaller than it is.

In a similar vein, another student included the following suggestion:

> To maintain the integrity of our can and counteract the internal and external pressures, it would be necessary for the can bottom to have a dome shape. Practically speaking, leaving out the dome would be disastrous in the long run and very costly (we're talking lawsuits here). Incorporating the dome into the design is beyond the scope of this engineer.

The Enormous Gulp

A unique design was an extended 12-ounce can. This student reasoned as follows:

> The current 12 oz. can design seems to fit the requirement for ease of handling. I was further assured that this was the proper size for the diameter of the can when I saw 20 oz. cans employing an elongated version of the standard 12 oz. can. Thus, my alternative design is simply an extended 12 oz. can that holds 15 oz. The mathematically-derived can looks like a can of dog food. If you have further questions, call my office at 1-800-GIV-ME-N-A.

Although I am not at all sure that this student did any calculus to come up with the design, he demonstrated some thoughtfulness and a justification that I felt deserved one of the higher grades.

The project receiving the highest grade did not even make a 15-ounce can. This student made a 30-ounce can instead and filled the container with two actual juice packs and a rotating top that permitted access to the straw holes in each box. Her argument appears below:

> It is R&D's observation however that the ratio of surface area to volume of the 15 oz. can is smaller than that of the 12 oz. can. In fact, on a range of optimized cans from 12 to 40 oz., this ratio drops significantly. R&D recommends therefore that the new Enormous Gulp be increased to 30 oz. 100,000 30 oz. cans would use far less aluminum than 200,000 15 oz. cans.

ANALYSIS OF THE DESIGN

Resolving my question of fairness and how to grade these unknown products was far easier than I had anticipated, perhaps because of the very visual way to compare them. Most of the accompanying written justifications from students were consistent with the physical models of the cans produced. Only the sphere-postulators were hurt by their written report. In addition, the quotes shared previously helped students in a few cases.

As I evaluate any new assignment, I have learned to ask myself a series of questions. Is this assignment a good one? Have my students extended or consolidated or applied what they have learned in a positive way? In the case of the Enormous Gulp assignment, my answer is not an unequivocal yes. The vagueness of the assignment—to minimize aluminum—made it difficult for the students to apply a known calculus technique. Although I think the students who really thought about the problem learned something, I am not sure that the majority of students were better off than if they had simply been given a traditional optimization problem. In fact, with a traditional optimization problem, maybe I should have included the requirement that they write to a soda company asking about can design in light of what we learned in calculus class. Past replies from the companies have been consistently wonderful. We lost this component, and I wonder if what we learned was sufficient to compensate for the loss.

CHAPTER *2*

A Scoring Dilemma

Recently, I began a new job teaching at a community college. Among my responsibilities was teaching a developmental arithmetic course. The students came from a wide variety of backgrounds; some had barely finished high school, whereas others had had second-year algebra but failed a placement test. Several had learning disabilities. They ranged in age from nineteen to their middle-forties.

A NEW ASSESSMENT STRATEGY

In the past, this course had been taught in an extremely traditional format. I wanted to strengthen it by connecting mathematics in meaningful ways to the students' lives, giving mental mathematics a high profile, building communication into the curriculum, and trying some assessment strategies from which both my students and I could learn. I created one activity called Think Twice. It required students to tell a story from their own lives in which they used or could have used mathematics. They were to pose a mathematical question and tell how they might solve it two different ways, using mental mathematics for at least one of them.

I pictured this as a regular assignment in which students could have control and show some creativity. I envisioned spending about half an hour in class every few weeks to have students share some of their stories. They could learn from one another; I could learn where they found mathematics in their lives and what mathematics they could do mentally. Also, I could offer third and fourth approaches that might expand their repertoire of strategies.

Early in the term I introduced the assignment, modeling for them real "Think Twice" problems from my own life. (See **fig. 2.11** and **2.12**.) I then made the first assignment.

FIG. 2.11

"THINK TWICE" EXAMPLE 1

Think Twice

I went to the automatic teller machine to withdraw $300. The machine gives $20 bills. How many should I have?

a. I could count by 20s to check my money: 20, 40, 60, 80, 100, 120, 140, 160, 180, 200, 220, 240, 260, 280, 300.

b. I know that 5 twenties makes $100, so I need 3×5, or 15, twenty-dollar bills.

c. $300 \div 20 = 30 \div 2 = 15$

A Scoring Dilemma

FIG. 2.12

"THINK TWICE" EXAMPLE 2

> **Think Twice**
>
> Marianne's was going out of business at a mall. There were lots of clothes marked 40% off. I saw a top marked $19.99. What would the sale price be?
>
> **a.** First I called the price $20. Ten percent of 20 is $2, so 40% is 2 × 4, or $8. When you take $8 from $20, you get $12, the sale price.
>
> **b.** I figured if you take away 40%, you pay 60%. Sixty percent of 20 is 6 × 2, or $12.

SCORING STUDENTS' WORK

I was disheartened by the first set of papers. Many students had simply mimicked one of the scenarios I had modeled. Several used such easy numbers that I doubted their problems—mostly about shopping—were real. I was not sure that they cared to do a good job. The writing was often difficult to decipher. Some students did not state the necessary information at the outset, pose a question, or even end with a question mark. Some never answered the question they posed! Nevertheless, I diligently made comments and corrections and scored the papers.

As a new instructor, I was learning about grading at the college level. Here final grades are recorded as 4.0, 3.9, 3.8, and so on down to 1.0, then 0.0 for failure. A grade must be at least 2.0 to be considered satisfactory. A typical grading scale was the following:

90 percent and above = 4.0

89 percent = 3.9

88 percent = 3.8

⋮

60 percent = 1.0

All details about assignments and grading must be specified in a syllabus distributed the first day of class. I knew that my mathematics colleagues usually had about 1000 "points" in a course. Within this grading system, I had decided that each Think Twice would be a 20-point assignment, so that five of them would be worth as much as one 100-point exam.

When I returned the first set of papers, one student was upset that she had "done what was asked" but got only 18 out of 20. I explained that I had been looking for reality, clarity, accuracy, coherence, and the use of mental mathematics. I then described examples. In my mind, I thought that I would give 14 out of 20 for satisfactory work, 16 for a good paper, 18 for an excellent one, with 20 reserved for an outstanding paper. This did not satisfy her. She also said I had not provided a guide sheet that stated exactly how many points each part of the assignment was worth. I talked to colleagues in other departments and learned that, indeed, at this college students were commonly given such guide sheets.

CHAPTER 2

A Scoring Dilemma

CREATING A RUBRIC

One English teacher used a rubric of 4.0, 3.7, 3.4, 3.0, ... as grades, the numerical equivalents of A, A-, B+, B, ... I wanted my grades to say "excellent," "very good," "good," and so on. I asked one social science teacher how she recognized exceptional performance. She said she might give 11 points on a 10-point assignment, but rarely. I thought, if I begin giving bonus points, then I have lowered my standards. Besides, I still had difficulty deciding what was worth 1 point, 2 points, or 3 points. I still thought 20 was something special, so I created a grade sheet to share with my students. (See **fig. 2.13**.) I also gave students the option to turn in an extra Think Twice assignment during the term to replace their lowest score.

FIG. 2.13

"THINK TWICE" SCORING RUBRIC

"Think Twice" Scoring Scheme	
18 points	State a real, personal situation involving adult-level mathematics.
	Pose a question, ending with a question mark.
	Answer the question using— ■ two different approaches; ■ accurate mathematics; ■ at least one mental math method; ■ a clear explanation of your thinking.
	(Note: If you can't use two methods, ask and answer a second question.)
20 points	All the above plus evidence of deeper thinking, for example— ■ three different methods; ■ very creative approaches; ■ source of the experience from reading or another course, not just consumer experiences.
under 18 points	This depends on the missing elements in the first list.

A Scoring Dilemma

CHANGING THE ROUTINE

I decided to change the routine for the second time I collected the Think Twice papers. I had students first discuss their stories at their tables, then choose whatever the group considered the best story to share with the whole class. We then listened to the selection from each table, thought together about the mathematics, and considered additional approaches. Students listened carefully to the selected papers. I sensed that they were impressed by the detail and thoroughness in some of them, as well as the reality and variety of mathematical thinking. Many students wrote more detailed and clearer stories the next time I collected Think Twice assignments.

I have collected, scored, and shared students' work on this assignment four times now. Since I presented the scoring scheme (and, maybe, because I write detailed responses on the papers), I have not had complaints about the scores.

But I also sense that some students feel defeated by my evaluations. More troubling to me is the fact that I struggle with issues of fairness, reliability, and the value of my grades as I score every set of papers. I still do not have a way to guarantee that each time I read the same paper, I will assign the same numerical score. If I take off points for each item on my scoring scheme, I diminish evaluations for students who do some significant thinking. If I cannot be consistent, then my students may be right when they say, "I don't know what you want."

Consider, for example, the paper about buying gasoline. (See **fig. 2.14**.) The student asked a good, realistic question, generally harder than other students would have tackled. He provided the given information and phrased the question clearly. Then he used paper-and-pencil methods (with errors) rather than mental mathematics as the assignment required. He did not explain his thinking or use a second method.

A Scoring Dilemma

FIG. 2.14

"THINK TWICE" STUDENT'S WORK 1

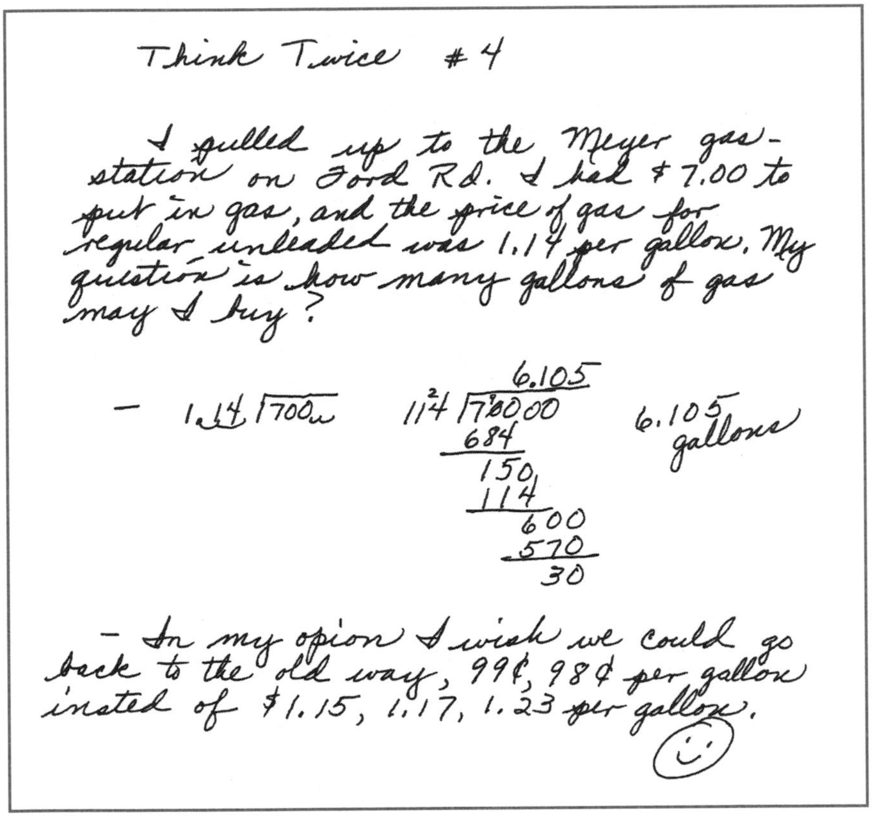

Think Twice   # 4

I pulled up to the Meyer gas-station on Ford Rd. I had $7.00 to put in gas, and the price of gas for regular unleaded was 1.14 per gallon. My question is how many gallons of gas may I buy?

$$1.14\,\overline{)700}$$

$$114\,\overline{)700.00} = 6.105$$
$$684$$
$$150$$
$$114$$
$$600$$
$$570$$
$$30$$

6.105 gallons

— In my opion I wish we could go back to the old way, 99¢, 98¢ per gallon insted of $1.15, 1.17, 1.23 per gallon. ☺

He did, however, close with a thoughtful point: it was easier when gallons were closer to dollars! So I gave him credit for the question and doing some mathematics as well as some mathematical reflection—15 points. When I look at it now, however, it seemed like a gift.

A Scoring Dilemma

Or take the case of the T-shirt story. (See **fig. 2.15**.) This story was what the students might call a "blow off" effort. He asked and answered a question and used mental mathematics, but finding 50 percent of 40 is not adult-level mathematics and $40 is not what a T-shirt really costs. My score of 12 out of 20 was low, but I wondered if I should have given any credit at all for this.

FIG. 2.15

"THINK TWICE" STUDENT'S WORK 2

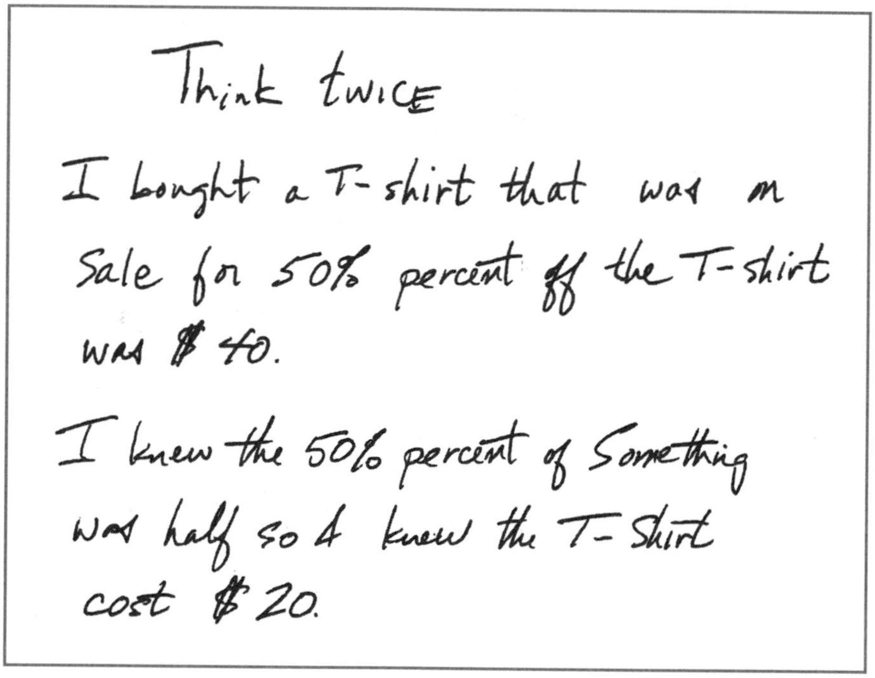

Think twice

I bought a T-shirt that was on Sale for 50% percent off the T-shirt was $40.

I knew the 50% percent of Something was half so I knew the T-shirt cost $20.

MY DILEMMAS

I have tried to use a "deductive and inductive" approach to scoring papers: first decide theoretically what I really want, then look at the evidence to see what I have missed and adjust my scoring scheme. But every time I think I can define what I am looking for, I read another paper that gives me a different idea. The variety of difficulties I encounter seems to be never ending.

Is my scoring scheme reasonable? Is it fair to expect something special for a score of 100 percent? How do I use points to score fairly, giving credit for good mathematical thinking and respecting a student's effort? How do I score equitably while recognizing wide differences in the backgrounds and abilities of my students? How do I communicate to students what I expect and then ensure that more students meet those expectations?

CHAPTER 2

I Just Collected 120 Portfolios—
Now What?

The hallway outside the mathematics department office was still choked with students on their way to the cafeteria. The members of the department crisscrossed the room, gathered food and folders of papers, and prepared for their regular Friday lunchtime department meeting.

THE DEPARTMENT MEETING STARTS

As most teachers settled in around the table, Sally, the department chair, began the meeting. "Let's get started. I thought we should talk about our portfolios today—with third-quarter grades due Monday."

Gail, a veteran teacher, responded. "Good. I just collected 120 of these things, and I don't know what to do with them!"

Dave chimed in. "I'm glad we're talking about this. Even though we've been doing portfolios for a while, and even though we talked about this before, I'm just not sure what to look at in these notebooks full of stuff."

Ralph, usually the last to join the meeting, rushed into the room and took the empty seat next to Dave. "Are we talking about portfolios? Good. Mine are so big, I'm not even sure what's in them."

USING PORTFOLIOS TO ASSESS

Over the last three school years, the Randolph High School mathematics department had been phasing in a new, integrated curriculum that asks students to compile a portfolio at the end of each six-week unit. Most of the department's members had at least some experience using focused portfolios that contain a cover letter followed by four or five selections. These selections were of two kinds: items chosen by the students to represent their highest-quality work or items specified by the curriculum because they represent important content of the unit.

From the beginning of this year, however, the department members had been wrestling with linking portfolios to the school district's move to standards-based assessment. They had discussed using portfolios that cut across individual units of the curriculum to document each student's growing understanding of the mathematics in each of the district's five content standards. They decided as a group that, at the end of the third quarter, and no matter where they were in the curriculum, they would ask students to compile and submit a standards-based portfolio.

I Just Collected 120 Portfolios— Now What?

PORTFOLIO CONTENTS

Dave turned to Ralph and said, "Did your kids include already-graded stuff in their portfolios? Some of mine only put in work I've already graded, so there's not much for me to do."

"What's the point, then, if there's nothing new for you to learn? I told my students to include only work I hadn't seen yet." But Ralph paused, and then said, "Now I'm sorry I did that, because my weekend is shot."

Sally spoke loudly to get everyone's attention. "I told my students to choose only five pieces of work, so their portfolios would not be huge. I guess I also hoped they'd have to think about what to choose if they could only choose one for each of the standards. From what I've seen so far, some didn't pick very thoughtfully, or maybe I didn't give enough guidance on how to pick. Do they need more help with what to put in these larger portfolios?"

Dana had been teaching for a while before coming to Randolph this year. She and Sally had spoken about this before. "Did any of you give students time in class to assemble their portfolios?" she asked. "I wasn't sure if this was a task they could complete on their own, so I told my classes last Tuesday to be ready to work on their portfolios on Wednesday. Then I started my Wednesday classes by describing the criteria we agreed to last fall—you know, an introduction, a cover sheet for each item, items for each district standard. I let them consult with their groupmates or me as they looked through their notebooks."

Dana continued, "In each class, there were lots of kids who seemed confused about what to choose, and now I'm not so sure myself. Do we want them to show growth or mastery? Should it be their highest level of work, or should they include some pieces that helped them develop their understanding, even if it isn't their best work? And there were lots of questions about how it would be graded. I haven't looked at them yet, so I don't know if the time I spent in class made any difference."

Gail's frown grew more severe. "I wonder how much the kids really understand why we want them to do these." She shook her head. "This conversation is not helping me."

CHAPTER 2

I Just Collected 120 Portfolios— Now What?

PURPOSE OF PORTFOLIOS

Sally spoke up again. "Maybe we should step back for a second. Do we all agree on the purpose of doing portfolios in the first place?"

Dave answered first. "I'm looking for the kids' best work. I just want to see their highest level of understanding of each of the standards. That's what we're going to have to report, so that's all we should be looking for."

Betsy, another of the department's veteran teachers, spoke next. "I'm hoping they will show growth in each kid's understanding over time. If the kids pick well each quarter, we should be able to see how much they've learned at each step."

"I thought portfolios were mostly for the students' benefit, to help them pull together their ideas and thinking," said Meg, a new teacher, who had not yet taught the new curriculum. "I never really planned to use them for anything."

"The most valuable part of this for me," Dana said, "has always been reading what the kids say about why they picked what they picked. Some talk about how much they learned, but some talk more about what is still giving them trouble. This has been really helpful to me as I planned for the next unit. I felt that, by giving kids the chance to talk about their understanding of math, along with their frustrations, I was really gathering information about what they know and how I could better understand their thinking. Unfortunately, I still have to assign grades."

I Just Collected 120 Portfolios—Now What?

GRADING PORTFOLIOS

Ralph put down his sandwich and interrupted. "If they're talking about what they don't know, then how are we supposed to assign a grade? And if we're not going to grade them, what's the point? I'd be surprised if any of my students would even do a portfolio if I didn't grade them."

Dana spoke directly to Ralph. "If the purpose of having the kids do portfolios is to measure growth, or to get kids to reflect, then assigning grades doesn't make much sense to me. Why would a kid reflect honestly about what she still has to learn if there's a grade at stake? There must be a way to get students to do such a valuable exercise without the threat of a grade."

Jane was a second-year teacher who had graduated from a college with a new program for prospective mathematics teachers. She spoke for the first time. "I tried portfolios like this at the end of first and second quarter, too. I used our four-level rubric to grade them, but I struggled with what it meant to 'meet the standard' or 'exceed the standard.' When we grade math problems using this rubric, meeting the standard has to do with the correctness of the answers and the ways they are justified. To grade a portfolio this way, meeting the standard would be more about how thoughtful the kids were in choosing items. How do you communicate that to the kids?" Turning to Dana, she said, "If we could do that, then maybe grading portfolios would make sense."

Throwing her hands up, Gail said, "I'm not convinced any of the kids get the rubrics we've been using now. I'd be afraid to redefine each of the levels. Maybe Ralph is right about only gathering the kids' best work and grading it accordingly. Maybe this is why it is so hard for me to get my kids to do these portfolios."

There was a pause as the group digested the conversation. Sally broke the quiet. "Here's what I've been thinking. I've been grading kids' work all along this quarter, so I have lots of information already. I'm hoping their portfolios will fill in the blanks by telling me things I don't already know. So, I'm going to look at my gradebook first, decide what I still need to know about a student, then look for just that in the portfolio. That'll save me time and tell me what I need to know, I hope. What do you all think about that?"

"I think I like that way of thinking about this," Betsy replied. "It's not like we haven't been assessing kids all along. But I'm afraid I'm going to spend a lot of time looking at my gradebook and trying to figure out what I do know about each of my students."

Dave said, "I haven't been grading much at all during this quarter. I thought I'd just look at it all in the portfolio. That saved me lots of time in the last nine weeks. So what happens? It takes me half an hour to read the very first portfolio, and the work in there is not nearly as good as I thought it would be." Dave leaned over and mumbled to Gail, "I'm not looking forward to the next parent night."

CHAPTER 2

I Just Collected 120 Portfolios— Now What?

CONFERENCES WITH STUDENTS

Jane took advantage of another pause to say, "I'm just finishing up my one-on-one conferences with my students about their portfolios and their quarter grades. I ..."

Ralph interrupted, "You've already met with each of your students?"

"Most of them. I'll finish the rest this afternoon." Jane continued, "I decided to spend time here at school reviewing portfolios with the kids one on one, in class, during their free hours, lunch, before school, after, whenever. I thought this would be better than lugging a box of portfolios home and reading through them by myself all weekend. It took about the same amount of time altogether, but I think my students and I both got a lot more out of it. Some of my students really understand the mathematics in their portfolios. However, I wouldn't have known that if I had looked only at their written work, without their verbal explanations. One of our department goals is to help the kids learn to communicate their understanding both verbally and in writing, so what better way to get at what they really know than by asking them to do both? And," she smiled, "my grades are almost done!"

Betsy said, "That's a great idea. I wonder, though, if my students would put much time into writing their cover letters if they knew they'd be able to meet with me."

MEETING ADJOURNED

Gail gathered a stack of books and papers, stood up, and spoke to no one in particular when she said, "I have class soon, so I have to go. Maybe we can have the next portfolio meeting at the beginning of the quarter rather than at the end."

Chapter 3

Cases about Using Assessment Results

Does This Count for Our Grade?

I have been miserable for most of the weekend. It is the end of the first grading period, and I have been struggling with report card grades for my sixth-grade class. The district requires us to give a letter grade to each student at the end of each marking period. The district even provides guidelines:

90–100 = A

80–89 = B

70–79 = C

60–69 = D

Below 60 = F

They, however, are no longer helpful to me. As my instruction has changed to include more thinking, reasoning, and problem solving, I have tried to change my assessments, too. It does not seem fair to give my students only quizzes or tests when much of my classwork requires students to explore mathematical ideas and explain their answers in writing. But those tests and quizzes were certainly easy to grade. The answers were either right or wrong, and the grade was the percent of correct answers. At the end of the grading period, I simply averaged the percents and converted them to a letter grade according to the district guidelines.

CHANGING ASSESSMENT

This year, I encouraged my students to explain their solutions to problems, the difficulties they may have encountered while solving them, and their feelings about the class. They did this when solving problems assigned for homework or for partner work in class. Their writing has helped me understand their thinking. I did not feel comfortable giving them a letter grade on problem solving though because I was afraid that they would not be candid the next time they wrote. Yet, they would ask, "Does this count for our grade?" If I said it did not, many of them would simply not do the writing, and others would make only a half-hearted attempt. So I began giving them a check for completing and handing in the work, a check-minus if they did not include an explanation, and a check-plus for a thorough explanation.

The same thing was true with group work. The only way some of the students cooperated was if they were assured that it counted for their grade. So I used a performance task checklist as the groups worked together. This helped make the expectations for cooperation and communication clear to them and helped me know whether or not the groups were functioning well.

I worked with the other mathematics teachers at my school to develop a four-point rubric to use for group projects and open-ended problems. All students had copies of the mathematics rubric (see **fig. 3.1**) in their notebooks.

Does This Count for Our Grade?

FIG. 3.1

FOUR-POINT RUBRIC

NOVICE	PARTIALLY PROFICIENT	PROFICIENT	ADVANCED
BEGINNER	SOMEWHAT SKILLED	HIGHLY SKILLED	EXPERT
■ The answer is INCORRECT.	■ The answer is CORRECT, but the work or the explanation is incomplete or does not support the answer.	■ The answer is CORRECT.	■ The answer is CORRECT.
■ The work or explanation is missing or shows no understanding of the task.	**OR**	■ The work or the explanation clearly and completely shows understanding of the task.	■ The work or the explanation clearly goes beyond what would be expected of a student at his or her grade level.
■ Reteaching of the content is necessary.	■ The answer is INCORRECT, but the work or the explanation shows good understanding of the task.	■ Diagrams, sketches, labels, and tables are used effectively in communicating the solution.	■ More than one strategy is used to solve the problem.
			■ The response is exemplary.
■ The goals of the task have not yet been met.	■ The goals of the task can be met with minor revisions.	■ The goals of the task have been met.	■ The goals of the task have been exceeded.

When students did a project or nonroutine task, they assessed themselves using the rubric. They drew boxes on their paper and put a circle around the score they gave themselves. I would also write the score I gave them on their paper.

Does This Count for Our Grade?

ASSIGNING GRADES

Now I faced giving them grades. All weekend I hardly knew where to begin. I had collected so many different kinds of assessment data: group projects, student interviews, notes about students from other teachers, self-assessment and journal entries, extended open-ended problems, and a few traditional tests. My students' mathematics portfolios contained many of these items. I sat in my den at home surrounded by piles of files—stacks of these portfolios. I started with Heather's work. Her portfolio cover sheet showed the following information:

HEATHER	
Homework and in-class work	√-, √, √+, +
Group projects	PP, A, P
Open-ended tasks	P, PP, P
Quiz	90%
Performance task checklist	
Self-assessment	

Looking in Heather's portfolio, I discovered a paper that I had scored three different ways—with a percent, a letter grade, and the rubric score of Partially Proficient. In the fall it was so hard to get the students—and their parents—accustomed to the rubric that I decided to use this transition method. Parents did not want to know if their children were proficient or partially proficient; they wanted to see a percent score and often asked how their child was doing in comparison with the other kids in the class.

As I looked through Heather's papers, I also noticed that her self-assessments using the four-point rubric were usually the same rating as mine. I remembered that this was frequently true for the ratings most of my students gave themselves. (See **fig. 3.2**.)

CHAPTER 3

Does This Count for Our Grade?

FIG. 3.2

HEATHER'S PROBLEM-SOLVING WORK

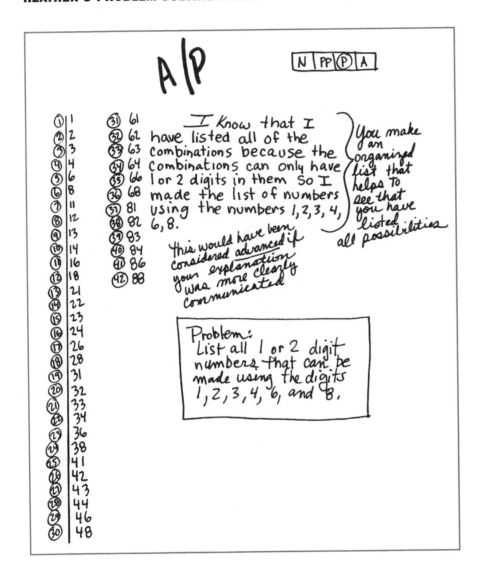

Does This Count for Our Grade?

Now I had to give Heather a grade. The 90 percent quiz was the only thing on her cover sheet that I really felt comfortable translating into a grade. (See **fig. 3.3.**)

FIG. 3.3

HEATHER'S AREA AND PERIMETER QUIZ

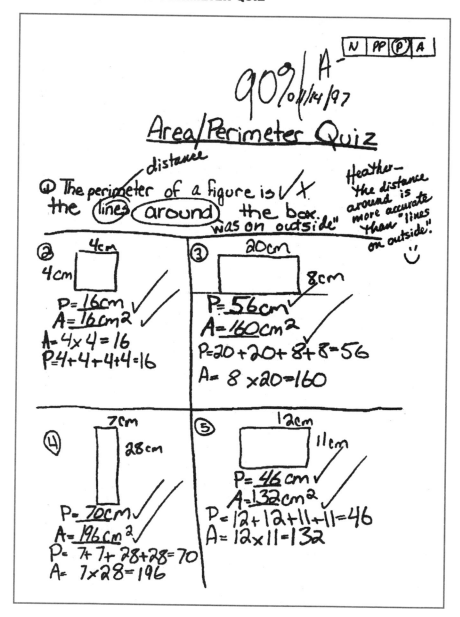

Does This Count for Our Grade?

How should I consider checks, check pluses, and check minuses in the average? How should I count the self-assessments and the papers with three different scores? Should the performance task checklist, used while they worked in cooperative groups, be part of the grade? (See **fig. 3.4.**) I knew that one way to get students to cooperate was to threaten them with a bad grade if they didn't cooperate, but when all these behavioral things are included in a grade, does the grade really show what a student can do mathematically?

FIG. 3.4

HEATHER'S COOPERATIVE GROUP CHECKLIST

PERFORMANCE TASK CHECKLIST

Student __Heather__   Date _____

	Frequently	Sometimes	Never
Approaches task in a systematic manner	✓		
Shows a willingness to try problems	✓		
Selects appropriate solution strategies		✓	
Accurately implements solution strategies		✓	
Offers assistance to group members appropriately		✓	
Accepts assistance from group appropriately		✓	
Organizes materials effectively	✓		
Demonstrates self-confidence		✓	
Shows initiative/leadership			✓
Thoughtfully considers the ideas of others	✓		
Perseveres in problem-solving attempts	✓		

Does This Count for Our Grade?

It was difficult and time-consuming for the teachers at my school to develop a rubric that they thought was equitable and that covered all cases, but now I have to figure out how to take those A's, P's, PP's, and N's and incorporate them into a semester letter grade. How do I incorporate Heather's response to Tony's Walk? (See **fig. 3.5** and **fig. 3.6.**)

FIG. 3.5

"TONY'S WALK" PROBLEM

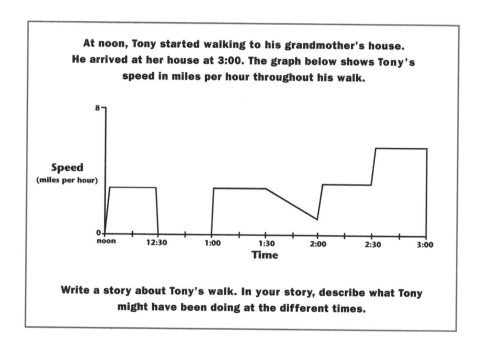

At noon, Tony started walking to his grandmother's house. He arrived at her house at 3:00. The graph below shows Tony's speed in miles per hour throughout his walk.

Write a story about Tony's walk. In your story, describe what Tony might have been doing at the different times.

Is Advanced a 100%? What if it represents work that has been revised? Is a Partially Proficient a 75%? Does a PP mean that the student has mastered 70% to 80% of the material? What is it? It's really hard to figure out what is equivalent.

I believe that assessment and grades are not synonymous. Information from assessment can be used for grades, but that is not its primary purpose. If a student gets a D, what does it tell us? When we talk about what a student knows and is able to do, that is assessment. If we go to all the effort of changing the way we assess and the only result is a more complicated way of coming up with a grade, I don't think much will be accomplished.

Does This Count for Our Grade?

FIG. 3.6

HEATHER'S SOLUTION TO "TONY'S WALK" PROBLEM

Now I have to incorporate all this information into a grade. I am worried that my students will no longer be clear about what it takes to get a good grade in mathematics. How can they be when I'm not? Understanding and communication are two of the many things that we are trying to include in the classroom. I have tried to establish a classroom where the students feel free to express themselves, to risk sharing their explanations without being laughed at, and to ask questions when they do not understand. Instruction has changed, and I have been trying to change the assessments to align with the instruction. But it's hard to figure out what to do with all these assessments at report card time!

Math Portfolio Night

My son Will, a sixth grader, is a good student who generally gets B's and A's without spending hours on his homework. Near the beginning of March, Will invited my husband John and me to view his math portfolio. Mr. Miller, Will's mathematics teacher, was holding an open house at school for parents to see the work the students had done in class so far. Will did not encourage us to go, but neither did he discourage us. "You can come if you want," was his uninterested comment.

PREPARING FOR PORTFOLIO NIGHT

During the week before the portfolio night, I noticed Will on the couch frowning at a bunch of school papers spread around him in a circle. Scissors and stapler close by, he was cutting small slips of papers and then stapling these slips to the tops of certain papers. He muttered to himself, and occasionally I heard a grunt or a curse. Although I tried to ignore the drama, after Will threw the stapler on the floor, I approached him and asked what was wrong. "This is stupid," was Will's heated reply. After asking a few more questions, I discovered that he was selecting work for his math portfolio, and for each piece placed into the portfolio, he had to attach a written comment to the top.

As he finished cutting and stapling, Will continued to complain, "Mom, it's a stupid waste of my time. I don't care why I chose this topic or any other assignment, and the only reason that I did the assignments in the first place was because the teacher told me to!" He was obviously bored and annoyed with the whole process. I was not looking forward to the open house, either.

THE NIGHT ARRIVES

When the night of the portfolio conference arrived, Will rushed John and me to the car, afraid that we would be late. Will seemed very excited as he jumped from the car and hurried ahead. Surprised, I quickened my pace while John called out to Will to wait for us at the door. Reluctantly slowing down a little, Will led us to his mathematics classroom. Brightly lit, the walls were covered with math projects done by the students. On one wall was a tapestry of tessellations, and hanging from the ceiling was a mobile of various geometric forms. Scanning the room, I was impressed by the wide array of media used and the obvious care that had been put into the displays.

Once inside, we found eight other students and their parents sitting at individual tables scattered throughout the room. There was a low hum of voices, as parents and students leafed through the portfolios together. Mr. Miller greeted us with a smile and shook our hands. Following a brief introduction, he started to explain the evening.

"Take about an hour to discuss the items in Will's portfolio," he began. "You will find the requirements for each item stapled in the front of the portfolio." He opened Will's portfolio and pointed to a description of the requirement for an assignment on fractions, which was a brief outline of the expectations for this particular assignment.

Math Portfolio Night

"This is going to be Will's night," Mr. Miller continued. "He will lead the conference, but feel free to talk with him about the items and ask your own questions." Mr. Miller then handed us a "scoring sheet" and explained that we were to fill the sheet out according to the criteria described by the general rubric (see **fig. 3.7**).

FIG. 3.7

PORTFOLIO EVALUATION SHEET

SCORING FOR DREAM TEAM MATH PORTFOLIO

4 – Excellent (evaluates and extends beyond all requirements)

3 – Acceptable (has met all requirements)

2 – Less than acceptable (has met most, but not all, requirements)

1 – Poor (has NOT met most requirements)

Circle the appropriate number (4–1) that corresponds to the achievement level of each category in the portfolio. Student-selected skills include geometry, fractions, formulas, computation, applications, organization, projects, and goal setting.

		Comment
1 Test/NBQ/or Quiz	4 3 2 1	_____
1 Project Rubric	4 3 2 1	_____
1 POD	4 3 2 1	_____
1 Writing Sample	4 3 2 1	_____
Proof of Improvement	4 3 2 1	_____
9 Weeks Grade Sheet	4 3 2 1	_____
_____	4 3 2 1	_____
_____	4 3 2 1	_____
_____	4 3 2 1	_____
_____	4 3 2 1	_____

COMMENTS!

Finally, please take the time to write a short note to your child telling him or her how you feel about his or her progress.

Math Portfolio Night

Depending on the items that Will had selected, the blank lines would be filled in from the following list of topics: geometry, fractions, formulas, computation, application, organization, projects, and goal setting.

"There will be parents and students cycling in and out of the classroom, so find a table and get started." Mr. Miller directed Will to take us to an empty table. "Oh," he added, "and please let me know about any suggestions you may have to make the conference better next time around." Mr. Miller left us, still smiling, ready to welcome the next group.

Will said, "Let's sit over here." He led us to a table in the center of the room. From the beginning, it became clear to me that this was indeed Will's night. Will would be the center of attention, not the teacher, as happens in many open houses.

Seated across from us at the table, Will opened his portfolio and presented us with a list of topics by subject area—an example of a test, an essay, and a homework assignment. After viewing a topic and requirements, we read his comment from the focus card and discussed the topic. Then, using the rubric, we rated each of the topics, filling out the scoring sheet that would be turned into Mr. Miller at the end of the evening.

Will's comments answered such questions as these:

> *"Why did I choose this work to represent a test?"*
>
> *"Why did I choose this particular piece of homework to represent my homework?"*
>
> *"What did you like best about this homework?"*
>
> *"What was most fun about this assignment?"*

On inspection of a few items in the portfolio, it became clear that Will had put minimal effort into his comments. Comments such as "I put this test in because I got a good grade on it" or "I put this homework in because I needed to put in a homework assignment" revealed to us little or no thought about the work or the assignment. Occasionally he wrote, "I liked doing this part of the math—it was fun," but when asked why, the answer was only, "It was fun because I got a good grade."

CHAPTER 3

Math Portfolio Night

Will did not know what to say or how to share his feelings about his work. My husband and I looked at each other and checked our watches. This was going to be a very long hour unless something changed. At this point my husband and I decided to ask Will our own questions, as his teacher had encouraged us to do. Out of college for almost twenty-five years, John started with a comment about a mathematics operation that looked foreign to him. He asked, "How do you perform this kind of math operation?" and "Why?" He then asked, "When do you need to use it?" Looking further into Will's work, we questioned some of his results, asking him to wonder, "What would happen if you changed this number?" Through our questions we tried to figure out why he found something more interesting, more difficult, or easier. We had him explain to us how things worked.

While looking at some of Will's work on area, John commented, "I had to use my geometry the other day when I was trying to figure out the best place to put up the dog pen. The problem was that I didn't want to cut down very many trees, but neither did I want to shovel off very much of the hill to make the ground level. I wanted to put up the fencing so the dog would have the most possible area to run around." Even John seemed impressed by his own ability to apply mathematics in the real world.

The idea of using mathematics outside the classroom continued to resonate with Will. The next assignment in the portfolio, a review on calculating percents, turned into a great discussion about percents and shopping. Using an example, we asked him to imagine that he was in a sports shop and found two hockey sticks at different prices—one stick was 25 percent off and the other 35 percent off. Then, if he could buy just one stick, assuming that the sticks are of equal quality, how would he know which one was the better deal? We actually priced a few sticks and worked through an example of how the percent deduction changed the price of the stick.

As we turned to each new section of his portfolio, we laughed and joked about Will's written comments and then dove into a discussion about the material. All three of us began thinking and talking about topics in mathematics that were useful and what appeared to us to be just mental gymnastics. Naturally, this was followed by a discussion on the value of mental gymnastics. We had a ball! It was a wonderful school experience, far more insightful for both of us as parents and our son than the usual open house.

Math Portfolio Night

Winding up the hour, John and I completed the scoring sheet Mr. Miller had given us earlier. At the bottom was room for us to write a comment, which Mr. Miller would read and pass on to Will. Although we had expressed our opinions verbally to Will throughout the evening, we felt it would not hurt to again state our feelings about learning:

Dear Will,

Your mother and I have had a wonderful time at your open house tonight. Thank you for sharing your work with us. We could tell that you have put a lot of effort into your work. We hope that regardless of the career path you choose in the future you are fortunate enough to keep learning as we have been able to do. Learning has been one of the great pleasures in both our lives.

Love, Mom and Dad

REFLECTION

As we drove home that night, my mind reviewed the evening. It took a lot of work to organize such an event, and certainly the students had put a great deal of effort into creating the portfolios. I had a really fun time laughing and joking with Will and John, as well as discovering more about Will's life at school. I realized that Will and I had never talked about learning as we had that night. I also wondered about what other parents and children got from the portfolio conference. John and I were able to pull out interesting and insightful comments from our son through our questions. Would all parents have that ability? Are all students capable of examining their own work (or anybody else's for that matter) with a thoughtful eye? And, once the night was over, how many parents pointed out that the ultimate goal of the work in the portfolio was to learn, to gather strategies to be able to learn, and to use learning in the future—not just to get a good grade?

I thought about the many risks involved in holding such a night. If we did not have a good relationship with our son, the conference might have degenerated into an unpleasant situation, or at least remained a boring one. And what if a parent has an unrealistic expectation of his or her child or of the school curriculum? What if a parent disagrees with the teacher's assessment of the student's work? Gone wrong, the evening could be a frustrating and confusing experience for a child. Staring out of the car window, I wondered what, if any, suggestions I had for Mr. Miller that might help assure a successful conference for everyone.

I also wondered if Will's attitude toward putting together his portfolio might change as a result of the open house. Could presenting his portfolio at the open house be the motivation he needs to value the portfolio process? Maybe his effort in putting the portfolio together will be greater now that he knows that we are interested. I hope so—I don't think I can go through the preparation frustration again!

CHAPTER 3

The Next Instructional Move

I was about to begin a unit on statistics with my seventh-grade class. I decided to give students a task to see how they approached a data analysis problem. I expected that the information I gathered would help me plan the upcoming unit. I decided to use Best Guess II[1] (see **fig. 3.8**) as an initial activity.

FIG. 3.8

BEST GUESS II PROBLEM

BEST GUESS II

The aim of this assessment is to provide the opportunity for you to—

■ choose appropriate statistical tools;

■ apply statistical tools accurately;

■ analyze data and use results to draw and support conclusions.

Gilligan, Skipper, and Ginger were trying to see who could make the closest estimate of when a 30-second interval had passed. They took turns with one of them guessing when 30 seconds had passed and someone else keeping time with a stopwatch.

When it was Gilligan's turn at guessing, the following times were recorded from the stopwatch.

31   25   32   27   28

When it was Skipper's turn at guessing, the following times were recorded from the stopwatch.

37   19   40   36   22

When it was Ginger's turn at guessing, the following times were recorded from the stopwatch.

32   38   24   32   32

1. Who do you think is best at estimating 30 seconds?

2. Give reasons for your choice.

Balanced Assessment Task 3080©

---

1. This task was developed by the Balanced Assessment for the Mathematics Curriculum Project. Funded by the National Science Foundation, design teams at Berkeley, Harvard, Michigan State, and the Shell Centre for Mathematical Education have developed high-quality performance assessment tasks at (roughly) grades 4, 8, 10, and 12 and assembled them into balanced packages of eight to ten hours of assessment. Two packages at each level are published by Dale Seymour. Best Guess appears in *Middle Grades Assessment Package MI*.

The Next Instructional Move

This was a new task for me, so I was not sure what students would do with it. But I thought the task had potential for me to learn what statistical tools students use to analyze a data set and what they take into account in drawing conclusions based on their analyses.

ASSIGNING THE TASK

I passed out the task to the students, and we read the problem aloud. I noted in particular that they needed to give reasons for the choices they made about who was best at estimating when 30 seconds had gone by. Then I had them work individually on the task. When I thought they had sufficient time, I brought the class together to share how they solved the problem. I had not looked at their written work, so the ensuing conversation gave me my first glimpse into their reasoning about the problem.

CLASS DISCUSSION

I began by taking a count of how many students thought Gilligan, Skipper, or Ginger was best at estimating 30 seconds. Fifteen thought Gilligan was best; five chose Skipper; and two chose Ginger. Then I asked them to share how they made their decision. I called first on the students who thought Gilligan was the best.

Tom: When I first looked at the paper, I looked at all the averages.

Teacher: You looked at the averages?

Tom: Yah, well not the averages, but the guesses that they had. What I did for Gilligan was I took the difference from each guess compared to 30 and then I added them all up and Gilligan had the lowest with 13. And, uh, the others, I think Skipper had something like 42 and Ginger had like 20.

Teacher: Did anyone who chose Gilligan have a different way of thinking about it?

Tracy: I rounded off each person's, um, guess, and, um, his were closer to 30.

Teacher: What do you mean by rounding them off?

Tracy: Like, I mean like, his 32 I rounded down to 30 and like one of 'em had 38 or something and so I rounded it to 40 and that was too high.

Teacher: And then you did what?

Tracy: And then I looked at whose was closest.

Teacher: Does anyone else have another way to think about this? Betsy?

Betsy: I looked at all the tries, like all the first tries, and then the second tries, and on each one Gilligan was closer to 30 than any of 'em.

The Next Instructional Move

When no other students volunteered to share how they chose Gilligan, I asked someone to explain how he or she decided that Skipper was the best guesser.

Chuck: I chose Skipper because I averaged all of the times that they had and when I averaged them out, um, Skipper was closest.

Teacher: Okay. Anything else to add to that?

John: What I did, okay, I did 30 seconds times 5 and so that would be 150 seconds altogether, right? So when I added 'em all up, and Skipper was closest to 150.

Next, I asked about those who chose Ginger.

Teacher: Richard, I think you said you picked Ginger for the best guess. What made you decide that way?

Richard: It just looked like it.

Teacher: What do you mean it just looked like it?

Richard: I mean, if you took 38 and 24 and added the 8 over 30 to the 24, it equals 32, so all the rest are 32 and one 30. If you did that with the others, they were, you know, further away from 30.

Harold: She was more consistent. Like Skipper'd be 19 and then he'd be way up on the 30s.

The class period was about to end. The students wanted to know who was right, and they wanted me to tell them. I said I would not tell them but that we would return to the problem tomorrow. I collected their written work so that I could look at it before our next class.

REVIEWING THE WORK

After class, I looked at students' written work on the task. I noticed that Tom's method of finding the difference between each guess and 30 seconds and then adding up those differences was an approach that four other students used. I wondered how Tom and the others decided on this approach and why they thought it was a reasonable method to choose the best guesser.

I found other ways that students thought about the problem that they had not volunteered in the discussion. For example, Sherill chose Gilligan and wrote:

> In all of Gilligan's guesses, the farthest from 30 that he ever was, was only 5 seconds. While Skipper had a guess that was 11 seconds away from 30 and one that was 10 seconds away. Ginger was closer than Skipper but she had a guess that was 8 seconds away and one 6 seconds away.

In a way, her method was similar to Tom's, but she seemed to be paying particular attention to guesses that were far from 30.

The Next Instructional Move

Denise also chose Gilligan. She had rearranged the times for each person from smallest to largest and circled the time in the middle. She wrote:

Gilligan	25	27	28	31	32
Skipper	19	22	36	37	40
Ginger	24	32	32	32	38

Gilligan's average was 28 seconds and he only went 2 seconds above 30 and 5 seconds below it. Skipper's guesses were between 19–40 seconds and were the farthest off. Ginger's guesses were between 24 and 38 but she kept going over.

James had calculated the mean, median, and mode for each set of guesses, displayed them in a chart, and then selected Ginger because she was the most consistent.

In looking at students' written responses to the task, I was encouraged to see that every student had some analytical tools to bring to the situation. At the same time, I was puzzled about a number of things. I noted that some students seemed to consider only one aspect of the data. For example, the reason students gave for selecting Skipper was that the mean of his guesses was closest to 30. They seemed to ignore the spread of Skipper's guesses. Why was there a tendency for students simply to calculate the mean when presented with a data set? I wondered what James saw in his table that led to his conclusion that Ginger was most consistent.

WHAT NOW?

At this point I had quite a bit of information about how students approached the problem. What I was still left wondering about was why they used the approaches they did, why they chose to attend to certain features of the data and not others, and if they considered whether their approaches and choices were reasonable. I thought back to our whole-class discussion. I really had no more information from that conversation than I had from looking at students' written work. What kind of questions had I asked? Why were the students looking to me to tell them who were right?

I'm thinking about where to go next. If I want my students to make sense of what others have done, or to consider whether strategies and solutions are reasonable, how do I do this through our class discussions? I worry whether our classroom is a safe enough place to allow students' ideas to be exposed for others to evaluate.

The Next Instructional Move

How can I revisit Best Guess II so that together we can consider the strengths and weaknesses of the various ways students reasoned about the problem? Since several of the students based their decision on the mean or median, I thought of posing the following question:

Suppose that each of the three was to get one more turn at estimating 30 seconds. Who do you think is likely to guess closest to 30? On what basis do you think that?

This question might get the idea of consistency back into the conversation for closer examination.

I'm not sure yet where to go next in planning the statistics unit. I do know that I need more information about how students are reasoning about this problem in particular, and any next step will be aimed at doing that.

Chapter 4

Facilitator Guidelines and Notes

Guidelines for Facilitating Cases

Using cases to conduct professional development requires that a leader, or facilitator, assume a very specific role. The facilitator's role is to ensure that discussions are rich and that issues are addressed in an open, constructive way.

In leading case discussions, facilitators will often need to ask the group to clarify issues to ensure understanding and to encourage opinions and solutions. It is not the role of facilitators to endorse or promote particular beliefs or opinions but to help participants come to informed conclusions. They must be aware of the needs of the group, be knowledgeable of the issues in the cases, and be prepared to keep discussions moving along a productive track. Discussions must neither become negative toward the author nor dwell on an issue or concern of a very small segment of the group.

Following these general suggestions, we provide a set of specific facilitator notes for each case. These notes give a synopsis of the case, a list of issues we believe to be in the case, and a set of questions to promote reflection and discussion about the issues. The notes also include connections to the *Practical Handbooks* of the Classroom Assessment series and a list of readings pertaining to the issues raised in the case.

Despite these specific notes, facilitating cases will be a challenge. It has been our experience that no two discussions about the same case are exactly alike. We found that teachers raise many issues other than those listed in the facilitator notes. Our best advice is to be flexible but focused in facilitating discussions about cases.

We offer additional advice to help in preparing for and facilitating case discussions and in dealing with facilitation dilemmas.

HOW DO I PREPARE FOR FACILITATING CASE DISCUSSIONS?

A key to leading productive discussions about cases is preparation. Before the group meets to discuss the case, we suggest the following:

- Read the case at least twice. Each time write down the main issues that come to mind for you. For each issue, write questions or comments that you might have. Think about how you feel about the issues raised in the case.

- If the case includes students' work, study it carefully. Try to make sense of what the students were thinking during the work. Do any mathematics included in the case for yourself.

- Read through the facilitator notes of the case. Compare your issues with those raised in the notes.

- If you do not feel knowledgeable about terms or issues in the case, use the references cited at the end of the case to do further reading or discuss the terms or issues with a colleague.

- If appropriate and possible, ask participants to complete the prereading activity in the facilitator notes.

Guidelines for Facilitating Cases

HOW DO I SELECT CASES FOR PROFESSIONAL DEVELOPMENT ACTIVITIES OR CLASSES?

Consider the needs of participants of the case discussion (e.g., Do teachers want to learn how to develop tasks? Do teachers want to learn how to score open-ended tasks? Do teachers want to learn how to create rubrics?). Also consider the context in which the case is being presented (e.g., Has a new state assessment system been mandated? Do teachers in a school want to change or reach consensus about assessment practices? Do teachers agree on assessment approaches?). Think about how you will make sure the needs and context are addressed in the discussions.

HOW DO I LEAD DISCUSSIONS ABOUT THE CASES?

- If possible, distribute the case before the case discussion meeting so that participants can read and reflect on it.

- Begin the session by informing participants of the purpose and climate that you hope to achieve together. This means ensuring that all opinions and ideas are discussed openly and respectfully. Tell participants that your role is to help them examine alternative ideas carefully. Be careful about offering your own opinion or resolution.

- Ask all participants to read the case silently. Make sure they have had ample opportunity to read the case entirely.

- Encourage participants to take notes as they read. Simply suggest that they may want to write down their thoughts as they read the case.

- Have participants work in pairs to decide some of the issues raised in the case.

- As issues and dilemmas are raised, ask questions to help participants clarify the issues and dilemmas. (See facilitator notes for examples of these questions.)

- For large groups, consider having groups of three or four participants discuss what issues they see in the case before beginning large-group discussion. Smaller groups give every participant a chance to express his or her thoughts or opinion.

- Stimulate discussion by asking general questions such as the following:

  - What facts do we know from the case?

  - What issues came to mind as you read this case?

  - What dilemmas arose for this teacher?

  - What is this case about?

Guidelines for Facilitating Cases

- Sometimes participants will often want to jump immediately to a solution to the problem or dilemma. Keep the discussion focused initially on developing a sound analysis of the problem before attempting to solve it. When participants begin solving too early, ask questions such as, "What does Joe say or do that leads you to that interpretation?"

- Once an issue or dilemma is identified, probe for further discussion about it. Ask for opinions about the issue or possible resolutions to the dilemmas. Make sure everyone who wants to speak has a chance to do so.

- A visual record of the conversation can be helpful. Using a flip chart, overhead transparencies, or a white board helps keep track of the conversation.

- As the discussion winds down, bring some sort of closure to the discussion. How might the teacher in the case resolve the dilemma? How might this dilemma be avoided in the future?

- If participants fail to raise an important issue or dilemma, you might say, "What do you think about ...?" to raise it for them.

- Close the session with a debriefing of the discussions and perhaps a plan for next steps.

WHAT PROBLEMS MIGHT ARISE DURING CASE DISCUSSIONS AND HOW DO I HANDLE THEM?

In facilitating group discussions, challenges may arise. Some participants may not speak, whereas others speak too frequently. Some participants may speak derogatorily about others. Some participants may espouse beliefs and practices with which you disagree. *Exploring Classroom Assessment in Mathematics* by Deborah Bryant and Mark Driscoll and *A Guide to Facilitating Cases in Education* by Barbara Miller and Ilene Kantrov offer specific suggestions to resolve facilitation dilemmas. Some of the suggestions that follow were adapted from their advice:

If the participants expect something else from the professional development experience than discussions about cases ...

Talk about the two sets of needs openly. Offer them a compromise by giving them some of what they want in addition to discussing cases. For example, if teachers want to learn to create rubrics, do so before or after discussing a case about dilemmas that arise from creating rubrics.

CHAPTER *4*

Guidelines for Facilitating Cases

If a small group of teachers comes to the session with a specific agenda in mind ...

Listen carefully to their concerns, acknowledge them, and discuss them openly with the whole group. Work their agenda into subsequent discussions about issues and dilemmas.

If a participant is reluctant to speak or a participant tends to dominate the discussion ...

Divide the group into smaller groups of two to four participants. Give persons in the group two minutes to say what they wish. Keep time carefully and require that other participants listen carefully without responding. Ask groups to summarize the issues and dilemmas raised in the discussions.

If participants begin to speak derogatorily of the teacher in the case or other people ...

Focus the discussion on why the teacher or individuals might have done what they did. Are there legitimate reasons for their behaviors? What factors might have caused them to do what they did? Or, focus the discussion on solutions to the dilemmas rather than blame. Discuss what the teacher or individuals might have done differently.

If a participant makes a comment with which you disagree strongly or that is not in line with current thinking on the issue ...

Give other participants a chance to respond to the comment. Explore their belief about the comment, and ask them to provide reasons for their belief. Use the comment as a chance to conduct an experiment from the disagreement. For example, suppose a participant comments that writing in mathematics is a waste of time. Ask how the participants might conduct an experiment to see if writing in mathematics classes improves students' mathematical understanding or abilities.

NOTES FOR
"Tessellation Presentation"

CASE SYNOPSIS

A seventh-grade teacher develops a tessellation project in an effort to engage her students in the study of geometry. Each student creates a tessellation that demonstrates six geometric concepts: symmetry, congruence, similarity, reflections, slides, and rotations. The amount of time that this project required and the uncertainty of just what the students learned from it leaves the teacher questioning the merits of the project enjoyed so much by her students.

PREREADING ACTIVITY

Ask participants to create a tessellation using pattern blocks. Ask them to give examples of congruency, translation, rotation, reflection, symmetry, and similarity in their tessellation.

MAIN ASSESSMENT ISSUES

- Using projects to assess concept learning
- Managing time
- Using interviews and checklists to assess progress
- Using peer assessment
- Assessing students' understanding

DISCUSSION NOTES AND QUESTIONS

Using Projects

The teacher chose to develop the tessellation project as a means of engaging her students more actively in the study of geometry. Students created tessellations, presented them to the class describing the geometric concepts illustrated in them, and assessed their classmates' presentations. What could students learn from each phase of the project (creating the assessment, presenting their concepts, and assessing the work of others)?

Managing Time

Projects, by their very nature, require a substantial amount of time. The major concern raised by the teacher was the amount of classroom time spent on the project. Is the time justified in this case? What benefits might offset the amount of time needed for the project? In what ways might this teacher save time for the next project?

"Tessellation Presentation"

Assessing Progress

The teacher observed and talked to groups of students to assess their progress. What information did she gain from her discussions with her students? How did she keep track of this information?

The teacher also used a very explicit checklist in documenting students' progress. What did she assess with the checklist? What are the advantages and disadvantages in using a checklist like this? How might the checklist be changed to give the teacher more information about students' understanding of these concepts?

Peer Assessment

At the end of the project, students presented their tessellations to the class and explained the geometric concepts that were illustrated. What criteria did the class use to evaluate these presentations? What did the teacher do to help make this stage of the project so positive? How did students benefit from evaluating the work of their peers? What did the teacher learn about students' understanding from their evaluations of the projects? What are advantages and disadvantages of having students assess one another's work? Is this information important in the teacher's evaluation of the project?

Reliable Assessment

In listening to the presentations and looking at the tessellations, the teacher was uncertain whether or not some of her students understood the basic concepts. What made her doubt their understanding? Do projects like tessellations lead students to an understanding that moves them beyond definitions of terms? If so, how? If not, why? How could the mathematical concepts be developed more in this project? How could the teacher learn more about what her students know about the geometric concepts?

Assessing Creativity

Tessellations are works of art. What criteria did the teacher use to assess them? Are there other criteria that might be used to assess the projects? What are advantages and disadvantages in assigning points to specific components of the project? Should the degree of difficulty or complexity of the design affect the score? Are aesthetics equally important for projects like this? Why do you think her former students found this project to be their all-time favorite?

NOTES FOR
"Tessellation Presentation"

CONNECTIONS TO THE *PRACTICAL HANDBOOKS*

Topic	Handbook	Section
Assessing conceptual understanding	*6–8 Handbook*	Assessing Conceptual Understanding
Assessing projects	*6–8 Handbook*	Multiday Assignments
	9–12 Handbook	Projects
Using checklists	*6–8 Handbook*	Teacher Notes and Checklists
		Conducting Observations
	9-12 Handbook	Teacher Notes and Checklists
		Conducting Observations
Managing time	*6–8 Handbook*	Managing Time
	9–12 Handbook	Managing Time
Using peer assessment	*9–12 Handbook*	Promoting Peer Assessment

SUGGESTIONS FOR FURTHER READING

Clarke, Doug, and Linda Wilson. "Valuing What We See." *Mathematics Teacher* 87 (October 1994): 542–45.

Edgerton, Richard T. "Apply the Curriculum Standards with Project Questions." *Mathematics Teacher* 86 (November 1993): 686–89.

Fuys, David J., and Amy K. Liebov. "Concept Learning in Geometry." *Teaching Children Mathematics* 3 (January 1997): 248–51.

Shaw, Jean M., Conn Thomas, Ann Hoffman, and Janis Bulgren. "Using Concept Diagrams to Promote Understanding in Geometry." *Teaching Children Mathematics* 2 (November 1995): 184–89.

Shimizu, Yoshinori, and Diana Lambdin. "Assessing Students' Performance on an Extended Problem-Solving Task: A Story from a Japanese Classroom." *Mathematics Teacher* 90 (November 1997): 658–64.

Vincent, Mary Lynn, and Linda Wilson. "Informal Assessment: A Story from the Classroom." *Mathematics Teacher* 89 (March 1996): 248–50.

NOTES FOR
"Does It Measure Up?"

CASE SYNOPSIS

A teacher decides to try a new approach to teach a lesson on measurement. Moving away from a textbook to a hands-on lesson, she is pleased with what she has learned about her students' understanding of measurement. Now she wants to teach all her mathematics lessons this way.

PREREADING ACTIVITY

Look at how a particular middle school textbook treats measurement in its curriculum. What concepts and skills are taught and assessed? What do students learn about the process of measurement? Think about how the lessons might build new skills and reinforce previously learned skills.

MAIN ASSESSMENT ISSUES

- Changing instructional and assessment practices and sustaining the change
- Managing time for assessment
- Assessing students during classwork and discussions
- Linking assessment and instruction

DISCUSSION NOTES AND QUESTIONS

Trying Something New

In this case, the teacher tried a new approach for teaching measurement. She asked students to measure objects in the room instead of working from the text. What prompted the teacher to change her measurement unit? What did she hope to accomplish with this new activity? Did she accomplish what she intended? What did she learn from this activity that she might not have learned from the textbook activities? What might she have learned from the textbook activities that she did not learn from this activity?

Throughout the activity, students remained focused on, and engaged in, their tasks. What factors contributed to their behavior and positive attitude? On the basis of student surveys, students enjoyed the measurement activity. It appeared to be a welcome break from the textbook. What are the advantages and disadvantages of hands-on activities developed by the teacher?

Sustaining the Change

The teacher liked the results of her new instructional approach and the enhanced evidence she received about students' learning. She wants to change all her math lessons, but she is unsure how to do this. She needs help. What might she do to make her mathematics instruction and assessment more hands-on for other topics?

More Time

The lesson from the textbook took one day of class time, whereas the new lesson took two days, plus extension activities to complete. Do you think the teacher should have devoted that much time to the activity? Why or why not? What are advantages and disadvantages in using more time on a topic? What factors influence how much time teachers should spend with a topic?

NOTES FOR
"Does It Measure Up?"

Ongoing Assessment

Throughout the lesson, the teacher observed and talked with her students. She seemed to understand how well her students were doing. How did she gather this evidence about her students' learning? How did she respond to her students' questions? What mathematical understandings were uncovered? What other ways might she have addressed the questions from her students? What does the teacher learn from her students' questions?

The teacher continuously assessed her students' progress through observations and student questions. What were some of the decision points for her as a teacher? What other ways might she have assessed the progress of her students during class? In general, what are some strategies available to teachers to monitor individual students' progress during class?

The teacher never really answers students' questions about the mathematics concepts and skills in the lesson. How does she address questions from her students? How does this strategy affect her assessment of students' understanding and performance?

Instruction and Assessment

The teacher's new activity altered the way she assessed her students. What did she assess differently from previous years? What mathematical topics other than measurement did her lesson address? Why? How did the way she developed the lesson influence the way she assessed students' understanding? Conversely, in what ways did her assessment results influence her feelings about the lesson?

CONNECTIONS TO THE *PRACTICAL HANDBOOKS*

Topic	Handbook	Section
Changing assessment practices	*6–8 Handbook*	Getting Started
	9–12 Handbook	Changing Assessment Practices
Ongoing assessment strategies	*6–8 Handbook*	Conducting Observations
	9–12 Handbook	Conducting Observations
Aligning instruction and assessment	*6–8 Handbook*	Aligning Instruction and Assessment
	9–12 Handbook	Curriculum, Instruction, and Assessment
Teachers' role during assessment	*6–8 Handbook*	Teacher Roles during Assessment

---

SUGGESTIONS FOR FURTHER READING

Clarke, Doug, and Linda Wilson. "Valuing What We See." *Mathematics Teacher* 87 (October 1994): 542–45.

Stenmark, Jean K., ed. *Mathematics Assessment: Myths, Models, Good Questions, and Practical Suggestions*. Reston, Va.: National Council of Teachers of Mathematics, 1991.

Vincent, Mary Lynn, and Linda Wilson. "Informal Assessment: A Story from the Classroom." *Mathematics Teacher* 89 (March 1996): 248–50.

CHAPTER 4

"Open Car Wash"

CASE SYNOPSIS

At the end of a five-week unit on large numbers, a sixth-grade teacher poses an open-ended assessment task. The students and teacher had established criteria for quality work, and the students had tackled open-ended tasks frequently. The students' struggle with making assumptions to solve this problem, however, left the teacher wondering about the appropriateness of the task.

PREREADING ACTIVITY

Ask participants to solve the Car Wash problem: *A car wash advertises that it has millions of satisfied customers each year. Is this claim reasonable?*

MAIN ASSESSMENT ISSUES

- Using open-ended questions to assess understanding
- Determining the purpose of the assessment
- Determining teachers' roles during assessment events

DISCUSSION NOTES AND QUESTIONS

Open Tasks

After fielding questions from students about the task, the teacher began to wonder if the task was too open. How did the students react to the openness of the task? Openness in an assessment task sometimes causes ambiguity. What was ambiguous, if anything, about the Car Wash problem? How did possible ambiguities affect student performance on the problem? Can a task be too open?

The teacher stated that the students worked in small groups to figure out some of the activities. How might working in groups affect their work on the problem? How can teachers help students transfer the confidence gained with collaboration to confidence in their individual decisions?

Assessment Goals

The teacher chose a task that she thought would assess students' ability to handle large numbers. How did the assessment task differ from the previous activities on large numbers? What do we learn about Justin's and Danny's ability to handle large numbers from their work? On the basis of the teacher's previous large-number activities and the Car Wash task, what do you think the teacher means by "handling large numbers"? Does this task assess the ability to use large numbers and the reasonableness of large numbers? What aspect of large numbers is this task assessing?

Prompting Students

The teacher was caught off guard by students' questions about the task. She was unsure how to respond to their questions. What decisions did she make with regard to her role in posing the task? What were the consequences of her decisions? How do you decide how much prompting to provide students on open-ended questions?

FACILITATOR GUIDELINES AND NOTES

NOTES FOR
"Open Car Wash"

CONNECTIONS TO THE *PRACTICAL HANDBOOKS*

Topic	Handbook	Section
Open-ended tasks	*6–8 Handbook*	Assessing Mathematics Problem Solving
	9–12 Handbook	Open-Ended Tasks
Prompting students	*6–8 Handbook*	Prompting Students during Assessment
	9–12 Handbook	Conducting Observations
Planning assessment	*6–8 Handbook*	Developing an Assessment Plan
Teachers' role during assessment	*6–8 Handbook*	Teachers' Roles during Assessment

SUGGESTIONS FOR FURTHER READING

Charles, Randall, and Frank Lester. *Teaching Problem Solving: What, Why & How*. Palo Alto, Calif.: Dale Seymour Publications, 1982.

Charles, Randall, Frank Lester, and Phares O'Daffer. *How to Evaluate Progress in Problem Solving*. Reston, Va.: National Council of Teachers of Mathematics, 1987.

Edgerton, Richard T. "Apply the Curriculum Standards with Project Questions." *Mathematics Teacher* 86 (November 1993): 686–89.

Kroll, Diana L., Joanne O. Masingila, and Sue Tinsley Mau. "Grading Cooperative Problem Solving." *Mathematics Teacher* 85 (November 1992): 619–27.

Shannon, Ann, and Judith S. Zawojewski. "Mathematics Performance Assessment: A New Game for All Students." *Mathematics Teacher* 88 (December 1995): 752–57.

Socha, Susan. "Questions with Multiple Answers." *Mathematics Teacher* 84 (November 1991): 638–40.

CHAPTER *4*

"Where Did That Question Come From?"

CASE SYNOPSIS

A group of teachers select what they consider to be a good assessment task on area and perimeter. They plan to give the task to their seventh-grade students and meet again to discuss if the task was a good assessment. One teacher is surprised that several of her students become confused when asked to draw rectangles on dotted paper. She questions the task as well as her role in administering it. She thinks about what might have contributed to her students' confusion.

PREREADING ACTIVITY

Ask participants to work the area-perimeter problem on their own. Have them think about whether or not this task is a good assessment of area and perimeter.

MAIN ASSESSMENT ISSUES

- Defining the teacher's role in administering assessment tasks
- Evaluating how well a task assesses what it is supposed to assess
- Using tasks with different representations

DISCUSSION NOTES AND QUESTIONS

Helping Students

This teacher was reluctant to help Jackie, who was having difficulty with the task. What did she decide to do? The teacher suggested several possible responses to Jackie's confusion. What do you think about these suggestions? What other ways might she have responded to Jackie's question?

The teacher had a particular purpose in giving the task to her students. What was it? How does the purpose of the assessment influence how much and how often teachers should help students?

The teacher decided not to help Jackie or the other students. How much help should teachers provide students during an assessment task? How would her help have affected her ability to learn about her students' understanding? What are advantages and disadvantages of not providing help when students ask?

Helping or Clarifying

The teacher decided not to clarify the task for her students. Should teachers help students if they misinterpret a problem? What is the difference between clarifying a problem and helping students solve a problem? What role does correctly interpreting the problem play in solving it? Should we help students who do not understand important words in a problem? Do we define mathematical terms for them during an assessment? What are advantages and disadvantages of clarifying problems and terms for students?

Evaluating Tasks

The group of teachers met initially to determine if tasks were effective. What criteria might be used to determine whether tasks are effective? According to these criteria, is this task effective?

Did this task assess students' understanding of perimeter and area? How or how not? If not, how might the task be revised? What other tasks might be used to assess understanding of area and perimeter?

NOTES FOR
"Where Did That Question Come From?"

Differences in Tasks

Some students seemed confused by using dot paper to show area and perimeter. Did those students understand perimeter and area? Did the dots interfere with the teacher's ability to assess students' understanding? Should students who really understand area and perimeter be able to use the dots in this task? How might the context of this task be changed to avoid their confusion?

When tasks ask students to represent a concept in a different way, some students may become confused. For example, authentic, real-life problems sometimes provide information that confuses students. Should teachers seek to eliminate confusion in tasks? How closely should assessment tasks reflect what the students had learned in previous experiences? What strategies might teachers use to deal with the confusion caused by open tasks? What are the advantages and disadvantages in using tasks with different representations?

CONNECTIONS TO THE *PRACTICAL HANDBOOKS*

Topic	Handbook	Section
Aligning instruction and assessment	*6–8 Handbook*	Aligning Instruction and Assessment
	9–12 Handbook	Curriculum, Instruction, and Assessment
Teachers' role during assessment	*6–8 Handbook*	Teacher Roles during Assessment
Prompting students	*6–8 Handbook*	Prompting Students during Assessment
	9–12 Handbook	Conducting Observations
Finding good assessment tasks	*6–8 Handbook*	Finding Good Assessment Tasks
	9–12 Handbook	Finding and Modifying Good Assessment Tasks

SUGGESTIONS FOR FURTHER READING

Chambers, Donald. "Integrating Assessment and Instruction." In *Assessment in the Mathematics Classroom*, 1993 Yearbook of the National Council of Teachers of Mathematics, edited by Norman L. Webb, pp. 17–25. Reston, Va.: National Council of Teachers of Mathematics, 1993.

Charles, Randall, and Frank Lester. *Teaching Problem Solving: What, Why & How*. Palo Alto, Calif.: Dale Seymour Publications, 1982.

Sammons, Kay B., Beth Kobett, Joan Heiss, and Francis (Skip) Fennell. "Linking Instruction and Assessment in the Mathematics Classroom." *Arithmetic Teacher* 39 (February 1992): 11–16.

Zawojewski, Judith S. "Polishing a Data Task: Seeing Better Assessment. *Teaching Children Mathematics* 2 (February 1996): 372–78.

"Why the Graph Breaks"

CASE SYNOPSIS

After students explore the graphs of the six trigonometric functions, a teacher poses a question to her students. They are to respond in their mathematics journals. On the basis of what she observed in class, the teacher is surprised at the frustration produced by her question and by the lack of overall quality of students' responses. The teacher wonders about the question she posed, the information she got from her students' responses, and about their resistance to writing.

PREREADING ACTIVITY

Ask participants to respond in writing to the following prompt:

> Refer to the function $y = \sin(x)$ to explain why the function $y = \csc(x)$ is discontinuous at $x = 0 + n$ (n an integer).

Then ask participants to exchange papers with someone else. Have them read and discuss the responses.

MAIN ASSESSMENT ISSUES

- ■ Using students' journals as an assessment tool
- ■ Posing questions that elicit students' understanding
- ■ Scoring and interpreting students' writing
- ■ Improving students' capacity to communicate their thinking in writing

DISCUSSION NOTES AND QUESTIONS

Students' Writing in Mathematics Class

Some students in this class questioned the value of writing in mathematics class. On the basis of what you have read, why do you think the teacher wants students to keep a daily journal? What are some other reasons for asking students to write regularly in mathematics class?

Grading Students' Writing

The teacher offered three specific examples to illustrate the range of students' responses to her question. Using her grading scale, how would you score these three examples? In what ways, if any, would you modify this grading scale? Why? How, if at all, would you modify the question asked by the teacher? Why?

Frustration

Many students in this class behaved in ways that indicated that they were frustrated by journal-writing assignments. Why do you think they were frustrated? What are some ways in which a teacher could reduce the frustration that students experience when asked to write in mathematics class?

Why was the teacher frustrated? What questions were raised by the teacher on the basis of this set of students' responses? What other questions might be raised? What might this teacher do for the next class?

NOTES FOR

"Why the Graph Breaks"

Promoting Writing in Mathematics Class

The teacher was not satisfied with the responses of some students? What could she do to produce a higher-quality response from Nathan? What could she do to help Stephanie? What strategies can be used to develop students' ability to communicate their thinking about mathematics?

CONNECTIONS TO THE *PRACTICAL HANDBOOKS*

Topic	Handbook	Section
Writing in mathematics class	*6–8 Handbook*	Promoting Quality Writing
	9–12 Handbook	Student Writing and Inventories
		Promoting Quality Writing
Posing good questions	*6–8 Handbook*	Conducting Effective Interviews
	9–12 Handbook	Conducting Interviews
Scoring students' writing	*6–8 Handbook*	Scoring Student Work
	9–12 Handbook	Scoring Student Work

SUGGESTIONS FOR FURTHER READING

Ciochine, John, and Grace Polivka. "The Missing Link? Writing in Mathematics Class!" *Mathematics Teaching in the Middle School* 2 (March-April 1997): 316–20.

Countryman, Joan. *Writing to Learn Mathematics*. Portsmouth, N.H.: Heinemann, 1992.

DiPillo, Mary Lou, Robert Sovchik, and Barbara Moss. "Exploring Middle Graders' Mathematical Thinking through Journals." *Mathematics Teaching in the Middle School* 2 (March-April 1997): 308–14.

Mayer, Jennifer, and Susan Hillman. "Assessing Students' Thinking through Writing." *Mathematics Teacher* 89 (May 1996): 428–32.

McIntosh, Margaret. "No Time for Writing in Your Class?" *Mathematics Teacher* 84 (September 1991): 423–33.

Miller, L. Diane. "Begin Mathematics Class with Writing." *Mathematics Teacher* 85 (May 1992): 354–55.

Norwood, Karen, and Glenda Carter. "Journal Writing: An Insight into Students' Understanding." *Teaching Children Mathematics* 1 (November 1994): 146–48.

NOTES FOR
"Peer Assessment and Self-Assessment"

CASE SYNOPSIS

A high school geometry teacher incorporates peer assessment and self-assessment of homework assignments into her classes. She constructs a rubric, shares it with her students, and spends time at the beginning of the school year having students practice with it. After several months, she notes that more students are doing homework, and she sees improvement in neatness and organization. She has seen little improvement in the quality of their work, however, and she finds herself disagreeing with more of their assessments.

PREREADING ACTIVITY

Ask participants to write down what they expect from students on homework assignments. What constitutes acceptable performance and what constitutes unacceptable performance?

MAIN ASSESSMENT ISSUES

- Asking students to assess themselves and their peers
- Communicating standards and expectations for the quality of the work
- Using the results of peer assessment and self-assessment

DISCUSSION NOTES AND QUESTIONS

Quality Performance on Homework

The teacher designed a rubric to communicate her expectations. According to this rubric, what were the characteristics of an A, a C, and an F paper?

You have collected students' work on a homework assignment, and you plan to grade these assignments. Make a list of criteria that characterize an assignment for which you would give a grade of A. Create a whole-group list of criteria. What are advantages and disadvantages of this particular rubric?

Helping Students Understand Expectations

The teacher gave students a rubric to use to score the first homework assignment. What process does the teacher use to help them understand the rubric? What other strategy might the teacher use to help the students understand her performance standards?

Joe disagreed with the first homework grade the teacher gave him. According to Joe, what were his criteria for an A paper? Joe did not seem to understand the teacher's expectations. In what other ways might the teacher communicate her expectations?

NOTES FOR
"Peer Assessment and Self-Assessment"

Peer Assessment and Self-Assessment

According to the teacher, what are the benefits of peer assessment and self-assessment? What did she see as barriers to achieving these benefits? In particular, the teacher worried about students giving high grades to their friends. What strategies might be used to avoid this problem and other barriers?

Several months into this school year, the teacher observed that more students were taking the process for granted. Why might this be occurring? What strategies might be used to avoid this?

What other ways besides having students assign grades to their work and the work of their peers might be used to get students involved in assessment?

CONNECTIONS TO THE *PRACTICAL HANDBOOKS*

Topic	Handbook	Section
Peer assessment	*9–12 Handbook*	Promoting Peer Assessment
Self-assessment	*6–8 Handbook*	Promoting Student Reflection and Self-Assessment
	9–12 Handbook	Promoting Student Self-Assessment
Making instructional decisions	*6–8 Handbook*	Making Instructional Decisions
	9–12 Handbook	Making Instructional Decisions

SUGGESTIONS FOR FURTHER READING

Csongor, Julianna E. "Mirror, Mirror on the Wall ... Teaching Self-Assessment to Students." *Mathematics Teacher* 85 (November 1992): 636–37.

Kenney, Patricia, and Edward Silver. "Student Self-Assessment in Mathematics." In *Assessment in the Mathematics Classroom*, 1993 Yearbook of the National Council of Teachers of Mathematics, edited by Norman Webb, pp. 229–38. Reston, Va.: National Council of Teachers of Mathematics, 1993.

Schloemer, Cathy G. "An Assessment Example." *Mathematics Teacher* 87 (January 1994): 18–19.

"An Assessment Experiment"

CASE SYNOPSIS

A high school teacher is concerned about differences between her students' performance in class and on standardized tests. She conducts an experiment in which she asks several versions of the same questions, and she observes some striking differences in her students' performance from version to version. She wonders what caused these differences, what she can do to reduce them, and just what her own tests—and standardized tests—are actually measuring.

PREREADING ACTIVITY

Ask participants to solve the following problem in as many different ways as they can:

> *The Acme Long-Distance Phone Company charges 50 cents for the first minute of a phone call and 10 cents for every minute after that. The World-Call Company charges only 30 cents for the first minute of a call but then charges 12 cents for each minute after that. What length call would cost the same if you use either company?*

Ask participants to share different approaches. [Possible approaches include solving the equation $50 + 10x = 30 + 12x$; graphing the two-variable equations $y = 50 + 10x$ and $y = 30 + 12x$; or using a guess-and-check strategy.]

MAIN ASSESSMENT ISSUES

- Using a variety of question formats to assess students' understanding
- Preparing students for external tests
- Evaluating the effects of high-stakes tests

DISCUSSION NOTES AND QUESTIONS

Question Formats

Students in these classes performed differently on questions written in different formats. How do you think the way each question was presented may have affected students' responses? The teacher says that she would like her students to "... see past the form of the question to the important mathematical questions." How can we help students do this? What effects do question formats have on students' responses?

NOTES FOR
"An Assessment Experiment"

Analyzing Students' Responses

Most of the students in these classes did not use an algebraic equation to solve the third version of Question 1. Why do you think they chose not to use an equation to solve this problem? Two examples of students' work for Question 1 are provided. How do the two strategies compare? What can you conclude about the mathematical understanding of these two students?

An example of a student's response to the second version of Question 2 is included. What did this student do to solve this equation? From this sample, what can you conclude about this student's mathematical understanding?

Many of the students in these classes had a much more difficult time with the last version of Question 2 than with the first version. What is it about these questions that might affect students' responses? On the basis of your analysis of their responses to Question 2, what can you conclude about the mathematical understanding of each of these students?

High-Stakes Tests

This teacher is concerned about the performance of her students on external tests. What are her concerns? Why is her students' performance so important to her? How is she addressing her concerns? What else could she do to address them?

The teacher includes preparing students for external tests as one of her instructional goals. What is her rationale for this goal? What impact should external tests have on instructional goals and curricula?

CONNECTIONS TO THE *PRACTICAL HANDBOOKS*

Topic	Handbook	Section
Using tests	*6–8 Handbook*	Quizzes and Tests
	9–12 Handbook	Collecting Evidence through Tests
Altering assessment tasks	*6–8 Handbook*	Expanding Tasks
	9–12 Handbook	Finding and Modifying Good Assessment Tasks

SUGGESTIONS FOR FURTHER READING

Manon, Jon Rahn. "The Mathematics Test: A New Role for an Old Friend." *Mathematics Teacher* 88 (February 1995): 138–41.

National Council of Teachers of Mathematics. "This Is a Test. This Is Only a Test …" *Mathematics Education Dialogues* 1(May/June 1998): 1–15.

Shepard, Lorrie A. "Why We Need Better Assessments." *Educational Leadership* 46 (April 1989): 4–9.

Thompson, Denisse, Charlene Beckman, and Sharon Senk. "Improving Classroom Tests as a Means of Improving Assessment." *Mathematics Teacher* 90 (January 1997): 58–64.

NOTES FOR
"Right or Wrong"

CASE SYNOPSIS

A group of elementary and middle school teachers meet in a workshop on assessment strategies. They are given a problem along with two students' responses. After scoring each sample on a scale of 0 to 5, they share the reasons for assigning scores. As expected, the teachers have different opinions about how to score the work. Discussions highlight different beliefs and values that influenced their scoring. Recognizing the subjectivity in scoring the papers, the discussion shifts to developing and using scoring schemes as a means to increase the consistency in grading.

PREREADING ACTIVITY

Ask participants to look at the two samples of students' work and score them on a scale of 0 to 5. Have them write down their reasons for their scores.

MAIN ASSESSMENT ISSUES

■ Assessing students' work

■ Subjectivity and consistency in scoring students' work

■ Usefulness of rubrics

DISCUSSION NOTES AND QUESTIONS

Scoring Students' Work with Rubrics

The workshop presenters asked teachers to score two samples of students' work. What was the presenters' goal in making this assignment? How did the scores differ?

The workshop presenters asked the teachers to use a 5-point scale to score the students' work. The 5-point scale used by the teachers was not clearly defined. That is, specific students' performances were not assigned point values. Why did the presenters decide not to clearly define the 5-point scale? How might this lack of definition have affected the results? What criteria did the teachers use to assess the students' work?

A few teachers felt no points should be given because the answer was incorrect. They argued that mathematical answers are either right or wrong. Others thought students should be given some credit for making an attempt. What is your reaction to these points of view? How might teachers respond to colleagues who hold these points of view?

The range of scores for the tasks was quite large. Why do you think the range was so large? What role did the task itself play in the range of scores? What role did the scoring method play in the range of scores? What role did the teachers' beliefs play in the range of scores?

At the end, the presenters considered having teachers develop a rubric. How do rubrics differ from grades? What advantages or disadvantages do either have? Should rubrics be used to score any type of mathematics performance, or are some types of performance more suitable for using rubrics?

Students' Thinking

The students did not include an explanation of their work. How might teachers' judgments have been affected by this? How might the task be rewritten to reveal students' thinking more clearly? Is there a difference between assessing students' understanding and evaluating students' work?

NOTES FOR
"Right or Wrong"

Giving or Taking Points

Some teachers talked about giving points; other teachers talked about taking points away. What are the relative merits of each approach? What are advantages and disadvantages in assigning points to components of a solution, such as 1 point for showing competence in multiplying?

Subjectivity, Consistency, and Validity

The range of scores indicated that this method of scoring was subjective. What is meant by subjectivity in scoring or grading? What evidence is there that the teachers' scores might have been subjective? How might subjectivity be reduced and objectivity be increased in scoring these tasks? How might a clearly defined rubric decrease subjectivity?

Individual teachers seemed consistent in scoring the two responses. What is meant by consistency in scoring or grading? What evidence in the case might indicate that the teachers were consistent or inconsistent in their scoring? How might teachers improve their consistency in scoring students' work? How might a clearly defined rubric increase consistency in scoring?

Validity means that a score accurately reflects what the task attempts to assess. What mathematics was being assessed in this task? Did the problem do a good job in assessing this mathematics? To what extent did teachers base their score on the mathematics embedded in the task?

Purpose and Scoring

At the end of the discussion the teachers stated that the purpose of the assessment might affect how they scored students' work. What comments did they make that indicated that this was a concern? What are different purposes of assessment? How might the purpose of assessment affect the way students' work is scored?

CONNECTIONS TO THE *PRACTICAL HANDBOOKS*

Topic	Handbook	Section
Using rubrics	*6–8 Handbook*	Designing and Using Rubrics
	9–12 Handbook	Scoring Student Work
Scoring students' work	*6–8 Handbook*	Scoring Student Work
	9–12 Handbook	Scoring Student Work

SUGGESTIONS FOR FURTHER READING

Clarke, David. "Quality Mathematics: How Can We Tell?" *Mathematics Teacher* 88 (April 1995): 326–28.

Stenmark, Jean K., Pam Beck, and Harold Asturias. "A Room with More than One View." *Mathematics Teaching in the Middle School* 1 (April 1994): 44–49.

Zawojewski, Judith S., and Richard Lesh. "Scores and Grades: What Are the Problems? What Are the Alternatives?" *Mathematics Teaching in the Middle School* 1 (May 1996): 776–79.

NOTES FOR
"A Difference of Opinion"

CASE SYNOPSIS

A teacher works with a group of teachers to develop a set of assessment tasks and rubrics to use districtwide with a new curriculum. Interested in involving students in the assessment process, the groups ask students to score papers that had been previously scored by teachers. The teacher uncovers a discrepancy between the scores of teachers and students on one sample of a student's work.

PREREADING ACTIVITY

Ask participants to use the rubric included in the case to score the sample of a student's work in rectangular solids. Have them write a rationale for their score.

MAIN ASSESSMENT ISSUES

- Aligning curriculum and assessment
- Trying a new assessment approach
- Scoring students' work consistently and reliably
- Involving students in assessment

DISCUSSION NOTES AND QUESTIONS

Working Together

The school district decided to have all middle school mathematics teachers implement a new mathematics curriculum throughout its middle grades and use common assessment tools developed by a group of district teachers. What are the advantages and disadvantages to this approach to instruction and assessment? What barriers might they have to overcome to accomplish this implementation? How might districts or schools begin this coordinated effort to develop a common curriculum and assessment program?

These teachers developed common assessments for their curriculum. What was their purpose in doing this? What other types of assessment might they have used? What are advantages and disadvantages in having all students be assessed through a set of common tasks?

Developing Rubrics

In creating assessments for other teachers, the teachers developed a rubric for each task. Examine the rubric created for the unit on volume and surface area. What do you think about this rubric as a tool for evaluating students' work on the task? What other types of rubrics might be used? What are advantages or disadvantages in using specific rubrics for individual tasks or using general rubrics for all tasks?

NOTES FOR
"A Difference of Opinion"

Discrepancy in Scoring

The students and teachers scored one sample of work quite differently. What factors might have caused this discrepancy? What criteria do you think the students used in scoring the work a 3? What criteria did the teachers use? What information about students did this provide the teachers? What did this difference of opinion show the teachers? What role did interpreting the reasoning of the student play in the discrepancy of scores? This discrepancy might have implications in disagreements between teacher and students about grades. What, if anything, should teachers do to support or explain their grading practices to students?

Students Scoring Students' Work

The teacher involved students in the scoring process. What did the teacher hope to gain through student scoring? What did he find out about his students? In what ways did the students benefit from the activity? Did it affect their understanding of surface area? If so, how? If not, why not? Was the scoring a useful experience for students? Why or why not?

At the end, the teacher wondered if it is feasible to have students score other students' work. What do you think about this issue? How might student scoring be made more reliable and consistent? How might student scoring be used to improve students' performance and understanding of the grades?

Assessing the Assessment

The experiment concluded without students scoring the remaining papers. Should the teacher have allowed the students to continue scoring? What might he have gained from doing this? What do you think the group of teachers should try next in their effort to involve students in the assessment process?

NOTES FOR
"A Difference of Opinion"

SUGGESTIONS FOR FURTHER READING

Clarke, David. "Quality Mathematics: How Can We Tell?" *Mathematics Teacher* 88 (April 1995): 326–28.

Kenney, Patricia, and Edward Silver. "Student Self-Assessment in Mathematics." In *Assessment in the Mathematics Classroom*, 1993 Yearbook of the National Council of Teachers of Mathematics, edited by Norman Webb, pp. 229–38. Reston, Va.: National Council of Teachers of Mathematics, 1993.

Stenmark, Jean K., ed. *Mathematics Assessment: Myths, Models, Good Questions, and Practical Suggestions*. Reston, Va.: National Council of Teachers of Mathematics, 1991.

Stenmark, Jean K., Pam Beck, and Harold Asturias. "A Room with More than One View." *Mathematics Teaching in the Middle School* 1 (April 1994): 44–49.

Zawojewski, Judith S., and Richard Lesh. "Scores and Grades: What Are the Problems? What Are the Alternatives?" *Mathematics Teaching in the Middle School* 1 (May 1996): 776–79.

NOTES FOR
"On the Other Side of the Desk"

CASE SYNOPSIS

A teacher of discrete mathematics gives his students an alternative to a final exam—to teach a lesson to the class. He develops guidelines and a scoring rubric as students plan their lessons. Students present their lessons in pairs to the rest of the class. The teacher wonders whether his new assessment was successful.

PREREADING ACTIVITY

Ask participants to think back to the first time they had to teach a lesson to a group of students. Ask them to share their thoughts. How did they prepare? How successful were they?

MAIN ASSESSMENT ISSUES

- Providing alternatives to traditional exams
- Creating positive assessments
- Assessing student-taught lessons

DISCUSSION NOTES AND QUESTIONS

Alternatives to Exams

Although he was teaching a new course, the teacher seemed pleased that his class opted for the alternative to the traditional pencil-and-paper exam. Why might his students opted for this? What risks did he take in trying a new assessment? What advance steps did he take in trying to assure successful presentations? What might he do in the future to help students improve their presentations? How might a less daring teacher approach such a new technique?

What did this teacher learn about his students that he might not have learned through a traditional exam? Give specific examples from the case to support your answer. What information could potentially be lost by not administering a traditional final?

Extra Time

The alternative exam took a great deal of preparation (including class time) for both students and teacher, probably more than the traditional exam. The teacher wanted to continue with new lessons but changed his mind. Why? Do you think this was necessary? What are advantages and disadvantages in allowing students class time to work on the presentations? What considerations help a teacher determine if an assessment is worth the time to administer?

Positive Results

The teacher wanted to conclude the term on a positive note. Do you think this was an appropriate exam objective? Why or why not? In general, how important is it that students feel good about an assessment?

The teacher worked with students as they prepared their presentations. Using examples from the case, how did he encourage students to experiment and take risks in their presentations? What else might he have done?

Nana's presentation turned out to be excellent, but it may not have. From the case, what did the teacher do or say to Nana that might have encouraged her performance? How can teachers help students who lack confidence in their presentation or communication skills put forth their best effort?

CHAPTER *4*

NOTES FOR
"On the Other Side of the Desk"

Judging from their postevaluations, one might say that most of the students enjoyed the presentations. Why do you think students enjoyed the experience? What other opportunities might a teacher create to ensure positive assessment experiences?

Assessing Quality

The evaluation of the presentations involved a complicated system of calculations and percentages and included guest evaluators. What does the teacher communicate to students through his evaluation system? How effective do you think the evaluation process was? What, if anything, would you change that might improve the evaluation of the presentation?

Peer Assessment

The teacher was able to fend off a disagreement with Ramo and cited references to the peer and guest evaluations. What role do you think peer and outside opinions played in Ramo's reaction? What additional benefits did student evaluators bring to the assessment? What additional risks did student evaluators bring to the assessment? How might a teacher help prepare students to evaluate other students' work?

CONNECTIONS TO THE *PRACTICAL HANDBOOKS*

Topic	Handbook	Section
Trying new assessments	*6–8 Handbook*	Getting Started
	9–12 Handbook	Changing Assessment Practices
Promoting peer assessment	*9–12 Handbook*	Promoting Peer Assessment
Promoting self-assessment	*6–8 Handbook*	Promoting Student Reflection and Self-Assessment
	9–12 Handbook	Promoting Student Self-Assessment
Designing and using rubrics	*6–8 Handbook*	Designing and Using Rubrics
	9–12 Handbook	Scoring Student Work
Managing time	*6–8 Handbook*	Managing Time
	9–12 Handbook	Managing Time

SUGGESTIONS FOR FURTHER READING

Tonack, De A. "A Teacher's View on Classroom Assessment: What & How." *Mathematics Teaching in the Middle School* 2 (November-December 1996): 70–73.

Kenney, Patricia, and Edward Silver. "Student Self-Assessment in Mathematics." In *Assessment in the Mathematics Classroom*, 1993 Yearbook of the National Council of Teachers of Mathematics, edited by Norman Webb, pp. 229–38. Reston, Va.: National Council of Teachers of Mathematics, 1993.

Stenmark, Jean K., ed. *Mathematics Assessment: Myths, Models, Good Questions, and Practical Suggestions.* Reston, Va.: National Council of Teachers of Mathematics, 1991.

NOTES FOR
"The Enormous Gulp"

CASE SYNOPSIS

A calculus teacher gives her students a realistic mathematical problem to solve—to minimize the amount of aluminum in a 15-ounce beverage can—based on an article that describes the construction of a 12-ounce can. Although she has given a simplified version of the problem in previous years and has provided a clear scoring rubric, she chooses not to clarify her expectations for this problem. Students complete the problem at a variety of levels.

PREREADING ACTIVITY

Ask participants to read the instructions for the Great Can Project in the case. Have them explain how they might complete the project. What strategies will they use? What tools will they use? What mathematics is necessary to complete the project?

MAIN ASSESSMENT ISSUES

- Using real mathematical tasks for authentic assessment
- Communicating performance expectations to students
- Revising assessment tasks

DISCUSSION NOTES AND QUESTIONS

Authentic Assessment

The teacher changed a traditional problem into an authentic problem for students to solve—one that may not have a clean or best solution. What new variables did she introduce for both herself and students with the Enormous Gulp problem? How did students respond to the challenge? Specifically, what mathematical connections were students able to make while attempting to solve the problem? How did their connections fit with the mathematics curricula (in this case, a calculus course)? What are the advantages and disadvantages of using problems like this to assess students in a mathematics course?

The teacher noted the challenge of grading her students' performance on their can design. How would you assess the Enormous Gulp problem? What criteria would you use? What other challenges might teachers have in scoring authentic tasks like this? What are some of the advantages? How might a rubric outlining the expectations of the responses improve or limit students' responses?

CHAPTER *4*

NOTES FOR
"The Enormous Gulp"

No Expectations

The teacher gave a problem to students without explicitly defining her expectations. Why did she decide to do this? To what extent should students know in advance what is expected them? What kinds of expectations are reasonable? What are advantages and disadvantages of giving students tasks cold without clearly defining the expectations?

Although the teacher outlined possible responses before receiving the projects, she created a postproject rubric after reviewing visual and written overviews of the students' projects. What types of projects did she reward with a high grade? What types of projects did she give a low grade? What types of projects did she give a respectable grade? She decided to place the projects in categories and assign grades according to categories. What are the advantages and disadvantages of using this strategy to determine scores or grades?

The assignment description indicated that the student was hired because of his or her extensive knowledge of calculus. What role did mathematics knowledge play in the teacher's assignment of grades? Did the task itself encourage students to use their calculus in producing creative answers? Why or why not? What role did creativity play in the teacher's assignment of grades? How might a teacher encourage students to use creativity and mathematics to solve problems?

Revising Tasks

The teacher actively worked on developing a task that was both interesting to students and useful in gaining a deeper understanding of calculus. She admitted that the vagueness of the problem made it difficult for students to apply a known calculus technique. How might this vagueness be reduced for the problem? What is the value of posing authentic tasks that might be vague or confusing to students?

As the teacher reflected on her assessment, she asked herself a series of questions. What do you think of her criteria for a good assignment? How accurate was her assessment of the students' work? In revising the can problem, she developed an assessment without really knowing what students' performance would look like. What did she learn about her students through their work on the task? How can teachers develop and revise assessments in new areas, especially when they are unsure of students' backgrounds and abilities.

NOTES FOR
"The Enormous Gulp"

CONNECTIONS TO THE *PRACTICAL HANDBOOKS*

Topic	Handbook	Section
Using authentic assessment tasks	*6–8 Handbook*	Multiday Assignments
	9–12 Handbook	Projects
Communicating expectations	*6–8 Handbook*	Establishing Conditions for Success
	9–12 Handbook	Establishing an Environment for Success
Revising assessment tasks	*6–8 Handbook*	Expanding Tasks
	9–12 Handbook	Finding and Modifying Good Assessment Tasks

SUGGESTIONS FOR FURTHER READING

Curcio, Frances R., and Alice F. Artzt. "Assessing Students' Ability to Analyze Data: Reaching beyond Computation." *Mathematics Teacher* 89 (November 1996): 668–73.

Edgerton, Richard T. "Apply the Curriculum Standards with Project Questions." *Mathematics Teacher* 86 (November 1993): 686–89.

Shannon, Ann, and Judith S. Zawojewski. "Mathematics Performance Assessment: A New Game for All Students." *Mathematics Teacher* 88 (December 1995): 752–57.

Shimizu, Yoshinori, and Diana Lambdin. "Assessing Students' Performance on an Extended Problem-Solving Task: A Story from a Japanese Classroom." *Mathematics Teacher* 90 (November 1997): 658–64.

Warloe, Kris. "Assessment as a Dialogue: A Means of Interacting with Middle School Students." In *Assessment in the Mathematics Classroom*, 1993 Yearbook of the National Council of Teachers of Mathematics, edited by Norman Webb, pp. 152–58. Reston, Va.: National Council of Teachers of Mathematics, 1993.

Zawojewski, Judith S. "Polishing a Data Task: Seeing Better Assessment." *Teaching Children Mathematics* 2 (February 1996): 372–78.

NOTES FOR
"A Scoring Dilemma"

CASE SYNOPSIS

The teacher of a junior college developmental mathematics course reflects on the effectiveness of an assessment activity she designed. She hopes that the activity will be motivating because it connects mathematics to students' lives. She also hopes it will help her assess students' knowledge of mental arithmetic. Some students seem not to take the activity seriously, others write poorly, and the teacher struggles to give consistent, meaningful scores.

PREREADING ACTIVITY

Ask participants to do the Think Twice activity described in the following case:

> Describe a recent situation in your own life in which you used, or could have used, mathematics. Pose a mathematical question based on this situation, and then solve it two different ways.

Have participants share their responses in pairs.

MAIN ASSESSMENT ISSUES

- Communicating quality-of-work expectations to students
- Designing a scoring rubric for an assessment task
- Scoring students' work consistently
- Aligning classroom assessment with the school's grading scheme

DISCUSSION NOTES AND QUESTIONS

Encouraging Quality Work

The teacher was disappointed with the first set of Think Twice papers she collected. She did something different before collecting the second. What did she do? What were the effects of this? What are some other ways for teachers to communicate to students their expectations about quality of work?

Scoring Students' Work

The teacher used two samples of students' work to illustrate the difficulty she was having with assigning scores. Using her scoring scheme, what score would you give to each paper? How might the scoring scheme be revised? Why? What revisions might help the teacher apply this scheme more consistently?

The teacher wondered if it was fair to expect something special for a score of 20 out of 20, or 100 percent. What were some of her concerns about this? Why was the student in the case unhappy with her grade of 18? What are advantages and disadvantages in adopting this policy?

NOTES FOR
"A Scoring Dilemma"

The Influence of Context

The grading structure of the school and the schemes used by her colleagues influenced how the teacher in this case developed her own scheme. In what ways? What are your thoughts about how the teacher used the school grading structure and her colleagues' input to develop her scheme? How is the approach to scoring individual students' papers influenced by the grading structure used at a school?

CONNECTIONS TO THE *PRACTICAL HANDBOOKS*

Topic	Handbook	Section
Communicating expectations	*6–8 Handbook*	Establishing Conditions for Success
	9–12 Handbook	Establishing an Environment for Success
Designing rubrics	*6–8 Handbook*	Designing and Using Rubrics
	9–12 Handbook	Scoring Student Work
Scoring consistently	*6–8 Handbook*	Scoring Student Work
	9–12 Handbook	Scoring Student Work

SUGGESTIONS FOR FURTHER READING

Driscoll, Mark. "'The Farther Out You Go ...': Assessment in the Classroom." *Mathematics Teacher* 88 (May 1995): 420–25.

Stenmark, Jean K., Pam Beck, and Harold Asturias. "A Room with More than One View." *Mathematics Teaching in the Middle School* 1 (April 1994): 44–49.

CHAPTER *4*

"I Just Collected 120 Portfolios— Now What?"

CASE SYNOPSIS

A high school mathematics department devotes one of its regular meetings to a discussion of the portfolios they have just collected from their students. The imminent end of the grading period leads to a discussion among department members about the purpose of portfolios, the information they contain, the time it will take to grade them, and the method they will use to grade them.

PREREADING ACTIVITY

Ask participants to respond in writing to the question, "What is a mathematics portfolio?" Then ask people to share their definitions with the whole group.

Conduct a brainstorming session with participants around the question, "What are the purposes for asking students to compile a mathematics portfolio?"

MAIN ASSESSMENT ISSUES

- Defining the goals and purposes of portfolios
- Teaching students how to build their portfolios
- Making efficient use of teacher time to review portfolios
- Using assessment information gathered from students' portfolios

DISCUSSION NOTES AND QUESTIONS

The Purpose of Portfolios

Even though the teachers in the department had experience with portfolios, there still seemed to be a lack of shared understanding of the purpose of this new standards-based portfolio. What were some of the purposes discussed during the meeting? What are other possible purposes of portfolios? How does the purpose of a portfolio affect its form?

Guiding Students

Sally, the department chair, wondered early in the conversation if she had given her students enough guidance in assembling their portfolios. What kinds of guidance did members of the department say they had given their students? How much and what types of guidance is appropriate? How is the issue of guidance influenced by the purpose of the portfolio?

Grading Portfolios

At one point in the meeting, Ralph wondered how he would be able to assign grades if students showed what they did not know in their portfolios. What did the teachers say about the issue of grading portfolios? What were the reasons for grading portfolios? What are some of the effects of grading? What are ways in which portfolio grades can be used? How else, besides assigning grades, can the information contained in portfolios be recorded and used?

NOTES FOR
"I Just Collected 120 Portfolios— Now What?"

Portfolios as Communication

Jane described to her colleagues how she had been reviewing the portfolios with her students. Why did she do this? What were the implications of this for her and for her students?

Frustrated with Portfolios

Gail seemed to be the most frustrated member of the department. What caused her frustration? What other concerns were expressed by members of the department? What steps might this department take to refine their use of portfolios further as an assessment tool?

CONNECTIONS TO THE *PRACTICAL HANDBOOKS*

Topic	Handbook	Section
Using portfolios	*6–8 Handbook*	Collections of Work
	9–12 Handbook	Collecting Evidence through Portfolios

SUGGESTIONS FOR FURTHER READING

Asturias, Harold. "Using Students' Portfolios to Assess Mathematical Understanding." *Mathematics Teacher* 87 (December 1994): 698–701.

Crowley, Mary L. "Student Mathematics Portfolio: More than a Display Case." *Mathematics Teacher* 86 (October 1993): 544–47.

Johnson, Bil. *The Performance Assessment Handbook, Volume 1: Portfolios and Socratic Seminars.* Princeton, N.J.: Eye on Education, 1996.

Kuhs, Teresa. "Portfolio Assessment: Making It Work the First Time." *Mathematics Teacher* 87 (May 1994): 332–35.

Lambdin, Diana V., and Vicki L. Walker. "Planning for Classroom Portfolio Assessment." *Arithmetic Teacher* 6 (February 1994): 318–24.

"Does This Count for Our Grade?"

CASE SYNOPSIS

A sixth-grade teacher has begun to use new assessment approaches. She is faced with having to assign grades for the first grading period using district guidelines. As she changes her classroom assessment strategies, she is confronted with how to incorporate different types of assessment information into a grade. She is also concerned that the messages that grades convey to her students do not support her attempts to change her assessment system.

PREREADING ACTIVITY

Ask participants to think about the role of grades in their own education. Have them write a list of advantages and disadvantages to using grades.

MAIN ASSESSMENT ISSUES

- Differences between assessing and grading
- Translating evidence from assessment into grades
- Investigating the purpose of grades
- Communicating assessment results to parents

DISCUSSION NOTES AND QUESTIONS

Simplifying Complex Evidence

After changing her instruction to promote mathematical thinking, reasoning, and communication, the teacher gathered different types of assessment information about her students. What types of information about her students did she gather? What strategies might she use to interpret results from group projects, open-ended questions, performance checklists, self-assessments, and other work done by students into a grade? How might she include the work in Heather's portfolio and the scores on her cover sheet in her grade?

Heather's performance task checklist shows that she frequently perseveres in problem solving. Should qualities such as perseverance be translated into grades? If so, how?

Mixed Messages

The teacher was concerned that grades were a primary motivator for her students and that the students were no longer clear about what it takes to get a good grade. Is this concern valid? How might she convey to students her values about mathematics work, which include working cooperatively and communicating mathematical thinking, while at the same time give her students grades? How might she respond when they ask, "Does this count for our grade?" How might the use of different assessment approaches be aligned with grades?

NOTES FOR
"Does This Count for Our Grade?"

Assessing and Grading

This teacher used multiple sources of evidence in her classroom to assess her students' mathematics abilities. What evidence did she use? What is the distinction between assessing and grading? What are the purposes of each? What alternatives are there to converting assessment scores into a grade? What reporting schemes have you seen or used that convey the complexity of students' performance?

Communicating to Parents

As a way to get students and their parents accustomed to a rubric score at the beginning of the year, the teacher put three ratings on the students' work. What other ways might she communicate the purpose of a rubric score to parents besides translating it into a percent or letter grade? How might the purpose of new assessment approaches be communicated to parents? How might the teacher address parental concerns about the use of new approaches?

CONNECTIONS TO THE *PRACTICAL HANDBOOKS*

Topic	Handbook	Section
Converting students' scores to grades	*6–8 Handbook*	Scoring Student Work
	9–12 Handbook	Scoring Student Work
Communicating to parents	*6–8 Handbook*	Communicating to Parents
	9–12 Handbook	Communicating to Parents

SUGGESTIONS FOR FURTHER READING

Clarke, David. *Constructive Assessment in Mathematics: Practical Steps for Classroom Teachers.* Berkeley, Calif.: Key Curriculum Press, 1997.

Wilson, Linda. "What Gets Graded Is What Gets Valued." *Mathematics Teacher* 87 (September 1994): 412–14.

Zawojewski, Judith, and Richard Lesh. "Scores and Grades: What Are the Problems? What Are the Alternatives?" *Mathematics Teaching in the Middle School* 1 (May 1996): 776–79.

NOTES FOR
"Math Portfolio Night"

CASE SYNOPSIS

Middle school parents attend a presentation of their son's mathematics portfolio at a school open house. The evening is fun. The parents ask questions and engage in interesting conversations about mathematics with their son. One parent wonders how the evening might have gone for other parents and their children.

PREREADING ACTIVITY

Ask participants to discuss with a school-aged child what they like about their mathematics class. Have them ask about the students' best work and the students' most favorite topics or activities. Have them ask students how they use their school mathematics outside the classroom. Ask participants to write a summary of their conversation.

MAIN ASSESSMENT ISSUES

- Using portfolios to assess mathematics performance
- Communicating assessment results to parents
- Using questions to reveal what students know and like

DISCUSSION NOTES AND QUESTIONS

Mathematics Portfolios

Will spent a night selecting work for his portfolio. He placed items such as a homework assignment, a test, and examples of work about various mathematical topics. Do you think this was an effective method for creating a portfolio? What role should a teacher have in selecting items for a portfolio? What other ways might a mathematics portfolio be created? How might Mr. Miller encourage students to improve the quality of their portfolios?

Mr. Miller required students to use focus cards (the cards on which Will wrote his comments). What was the intent of Mr. Miller's focus cards? Did the cards serve this intent? What might Mr. Miller do in the future to help Will improve his written comments?

Will's mom reflected that "the ultimate goal of the work in the portfolio was to learn, to gather strategies to be able to learn, and to use learning in the future—not just to get a good grade." What were the teacher's goals in having students compile a mathematics portfolio?

Will's parents were asked to assess their son's portfolio based on a scoring rubric provided by the teacher. What do you think about this rubric? What rubrics have you seen or used to assess portfolios? What are advantages and disadvantages in having parents score their child's work? How might a teacher prepare parents to examine their child's work? What other ways might teachers assess portfolios? What are the advantages and disadvantages of using portfolios as assessment tools?

Communicating with Parents

The mathematics portfolio night gave Will's parents an opportunity to see their son's work and evaluate his progress in school. Was this consistent with Mr. Miller's goals in conducting open house in this way? What are advantages and disadvantages in holding portfolio nights in this way?

NOTES FOR
"Math Portfolio Night"

The insight and educational background of Will's parents helped them create an atmosphere of fun and learning for their son Will. Will's mother expressed concern that not all parents would have the ability to foster a lively discussion. What could a teacher do to promote this kind of discussion?

Do you think that the night provided the parents with appropriate information concerning the progress of their child in math? Why or why not? What other information might be made available to parents? What did Mr. Miller learn about Will through the conference that might be helpful to him as a teacher?

Questioning

Will's parents elicited interesting and insightful comments from their son through their questioning. How did they do this? Find some examples from the case. In what ways do the types of questions affect the assessment of understanding? Think of some examples from your own experience that demonstrate the role of questioning in assessing students' understanding.

Will and his parents discussed the value of mathematics and of applications of mathematics during the conference. They also discussed less interesting aspects of doing mathematics, referred to as mental gymnastics. How did Will's parents spark Will's interest during the conference? In assessing students' understanding, how important is it to pique their interest? Why? What role does students' interest play in assessment?

CONNECTIONS TO THE *PRACTICAL HANDBOOKS*

Topic	Handbook	Section
Using mathematics portfolios	*6–8 Handbook*	Collections of Work
	9–12 Handbook	Collecting Evidence through Portfolios
Communicating to parents	*6–8 Handbook*	Communicating to Parents
	9–12 Handbook	Communicating to Parents
Questioning strategies	*6–8 Handbook*	Conducting Effective Interviews
	9–12 Handbook	Conducting Interviews

SUGGESTIONS FOR FURTHER READING

Crowley, Mary. "Student Mathematics Portfolio: More than a Display Case." *Mathematics Teacher* 86 (October 1993): 544–47.

Kuhs, Teresa. "Portfolio Assessment: Making It Work the First Time." *Mathematics Teacher* 87 (May 1994): 332–35.

Lambdin, Diana V., and Vicki L. Walker. "Planning for Classroom Portfolio Assessment." *Arithmetic Teacher* 6 (February 1994): 318–24.

Robinson, Donita. "Student Portfolios in Mathematics." *Mathematics Teacher* 91 (April 1998): 318–25.

Stenmark, Jean K., ed. *Mathematics Assessment: Myths, Models, Good Questions, and Practical Suggestions.* Reston, Va.: National Council of Teachers of Mathematics, 1991.

CHAPTER *4*

"The Next Instructional Move"

CASE SYNOPSIS

A teacher gives his seventh-grade students a preassessment task on statistics to see how they will use data analysis concepts. He provides them with data from three guessers' attempts to estimate a thirty-second interval. He asks students to decide who is best at estimating the interval. The students must support their choice with reasoning. The teacher discovers that most students use some statistical concept to analyze the data. After a class discussion and looking at their written work, however, he still does not know why some students chose their approach. Using the information he gained from this activity, he is considering what the next instructional move for his class will be.

PREREADING ACTIVITY

Ask participants to work the Best Guess? II problem. In a discussion, have them support their choices with reasons.

MAIN ASSESSMENT ISSUES

- Evaluating an open-ended task
- Using classroom discussions to assess understanding
- Using assessment to guide instruction

DISCUSSION NOTES AND QUESTIONS:

An Open Task

The teacher gave his students a data analysis task. What purpose did he have in mind when he gave them this task? Did the task fulfill his purpose? What other ways might it be used? What do you think about the task as an assessment item?

The problem requires students to make a judgment based on data. Is there more than one best guesser or just one best guesser? Is any choice acceptable as long as students correctly explain the strategy used?

At the end of the class, students wanted the teacher to tell them who was correct. Why do you think he did not tell his students which answer was correct? What are the advantages and disadvantages of not providing them with a "correct" answer?

Mathematics of the Task

Part of the task is to determine what a good estimator is. In your opinion, what does that mean? Did the students' responses reveal what they thought a good estimator was?

In middle school the usual statistical concepts studied are mean, median, mode, and range. Which if any of these measures, either alone or in combination, were used by students to determine who was the best estimator? Did students use these concepts appropriately? How would you use them to determine who was the best estimator? What other statistical concepts might you use?

NOTES FOR
"The Next Instructional Move"

Describe the methods that the students used to solve this task. What are the merits and shortcomings of each strategy? Some of the students calculated the mean, median, mode, and range and used them to predict the best guesser. Others focused on how close the guesses were to a target number, showing an understanding of the essential question that was asked. What role did number sense or intuition play in solving this task?

Class Discussion

The teacher used a class discussion to learn what students had done. Describe the interactions between the students and the teacher during the discussion. What kind of questions did he ask? What did he learn from the dialogue? How did the students benefit from the exchange? What questions might he ask to get more information? What other ways might he have gathered this evidence?

The Next Instructional Move

The teacher considered what to do with the information that he got from the dialogue and written work. He concluded that he wanted to learn more about why the students selected their approach over others. He speculated that some of his students automatically calculated the mean because in the past that is what was expected of them. What do you suggest as the next instructional move? What experiences would help students realize that the selection of the appropriate statistical tool is as crucial in successfully solving a problem as the actual calculations?

The teacher suggested going back into the class and asking his students to look closely at one another's approaches. What are the advantages and disadvantages of having students review one another's work? What steps could be taken to make the classroom a safe place for such a discussion? How would the students benefit if they were asked to reach a consensus about good strategies or to reach agreement on who was the best estimator?

As a follow-up activity, the teacher considered posing the revised question, "Each of the three will get one more turn at estimating 30 seconds. Who do you think is most likely to guess closest to 30 seconds?" How does this question change the question that was originally asked? What kinds of responses might the teacher get to this question? What other follow-up questions might he pose to his students?

CHAPTER *4*

"The Next Instructional Move"

CONNECTIONS TO THE *PRACTICAL HANDBOOKS*

Topic	Handbook	Section
Using open-ended tasks	*6–8 Handbook*	Assessing Mathematics Problem Solving
	9–12 Handbook	Open-Ended Questions
Assessing classroom discussions	*6–8 Handbook*	Teacher Notes and Checklists
	9–12 Handbook	Teacher Notes and Checklists
Making instructional decisions	*6–8 Handbook*	Making Instructional Decisions
	9–12 Handbook	Making Instructional Decisions

SUGGESTIONS FOR FURTHER READING

Edgerton, Richard T. "Apply the Curriculum Standards with Project Questions." *Mathematics Teacher* 86 (November 1993): 686–89.

Lambdin, Diana V., and Clare Foresth. "Seamless Assessment/Instruction = Good Teaching." *Teaching Children Mathematics* 2 (January 1996): 294–98.

Shimizu, Yoshinori, and Diana Lambdin. "Assessing Students' Performance on an Extended Problem-Solving Task: A Story from a Japanese Classroom." *Mathematics Teacher* 90 (November 1997): 658–64.

Vincent, Mary Lynn, and Linda Wilson. "Informal Assessment: A Story from the Classroom." *Mathematics Teacher* 89 (March 1996): 248–50.

Wilcox, Sandra, and Ronald S. Zielinski. "Using Assessment of Students' Learning to Reshape Teaching." *Mathematics Teacher* 90 (March 1997): 223–29.

Wilcox, Sandra, and Perry Lanier. *Using Assessment to Reshape Teaching: A Casebook for Teachers and Teacher Educators, Curriculum and Staff Development Specialists*. Hillsdale, N.J.: Lawrence Erlbaum Associates, in press.

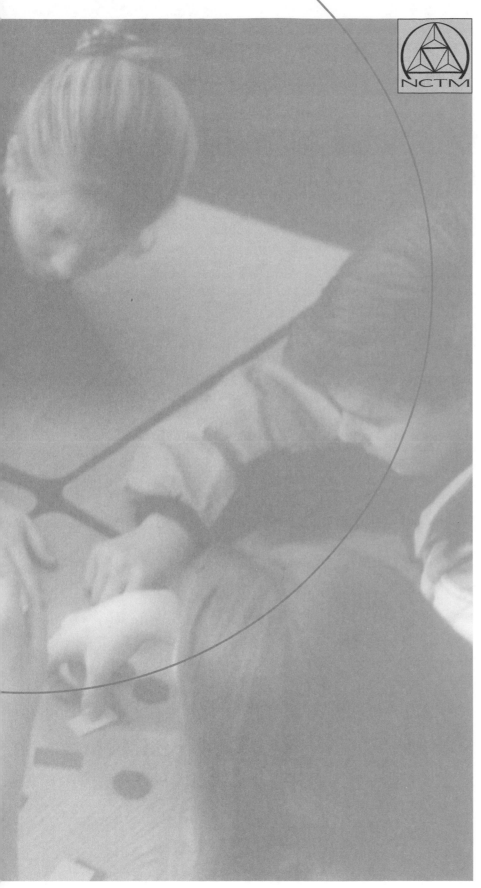

Resources

NCTM

Bibliography

Asturias, Harold. "Using Students' Portfolios to Assess Mathematical Understanding." *Mathematics Teacher* 87 (December 1994): 698–701.

Barnett, Carne, Donna Goldenstein, and Babette Jackson. *Fractions, Decimals, Ratios, & Percents: Hard to Teach and Hard to Learn?* Portsmouth, N.H.: Heinemann, 1994.

Bryant, Deborah, and Mark Driscoll. *Exploring Classroom Assessment in Mathematics: A Guide for Professional Development*. Reston, Va.: National Council of Teachers of Mathematics, 1998.

Bush, William S., and Anja Greer, eds. *Mathematics Assessment: A Practical Handbook for Grades 9–12*. Reston, Va.: National Council of Teachers of Mathematics, 1999.

Bush, William S., and Steve Leinwand, eds. *Mathematics Assessment: A Practical Handbook for Grades 6–8*. Reston, Va.: National Council of Teachers of Mathematics, 2000.

Chambers, Donald. "Integrating Assessment and Instruction." In *Assessment in the Mathematics Classroom*, 1993 Yearbook of the National Council of Teachers of Mathematics, edited by Norman L. Webb, pp. 17–25. Reston, Va.: National Council of Teachers of Mathematics, 1993.

Charles, Randall, and Frank Lester. *Teaching Problem Solving: What, Why & How*. Palo Alto, Calif.: Dale Seymour Publications, 1982.

Charles, Randall, Frank Lester, and Phares O'Daffer. *How to Evaluate Progress in Problem Solving*. Reston, Va.: National Council of Teachers of Mathematics, 1987.

Ciochine, John, and Grace Polivka. "The Missing Link? Writing in Mathematics Class!" *Mathematics Teaching in the Middle School* 2 (March-April 1997): 316–20.

Clarke, David. *Constructive Assessment in Mathematics: Practical Steps for Classroom Teachers*. Berkeley, Calif.: Key Curriculum Press, 1997.

———. "Quality Mathematics: How Can We Tell?" *Mathematics Teacher* 88 (April 1995): 326–28.

Clarke, Doug, and Linda Wilson. "Valuing What We See." *Mathematics Teacher* 87 (October 1994): 542–45.

Countryman, Joan. *Writing to Learn Mathematics*. Portsmouth, N.H.: Heinemann, 1992.

Crowley, Mary. "Student Mathematics Portfolio: More than a Display Case." *Mathematics Teacher* 86 (October 1993): 544–47.

RESOURCES

Csongor, Julianna E. "Mirror, Mirror on the Wall ... Teaching Self-Assessment to Students." *Mathematics Teacher* 85 (November 1992): 636–37.

Curcio, Frances R., and Alice F. Artzt. "Assessing Students' Ability to Analyze Data: Reaching beyond Computation." *Mathematics Teacher* 89 (November 1996): 668–73.

DiPillo, Mary Lou, Robert Sovchik, and Barbara Moss. "Exploring Middle Graders' Mathematical Thinking through Journals." *Mathematics Teaching in the Middle School* 2 (March-April 1997): 308–14.

Driscoll, Mark. "'The Farther Out You Go ...': Assessment in the Classroom." *Mathematics Teacher 88* (May 1995): 420–25.

Edgerton, Richard T. "Apply the Curriculum Standards with Project Questions." *Mathematics Teacher* 86 (November 1993): 686–89.

Fuys, David J., and Amy K. Liebov. "Concept Learning in Geometry." *Teaching Children Mathematics* 3 (January 1997): 248–51.

Johnson, Bil. *The Performance Assessment Handbook, Volume 1: Portfolios and Socratic Seminars*. Princeton, N.J.: Eye on Education, 1996.

Kenney, Patricia, and Edward Silver. "Student Self-Assessment in Mathematics." In *Assessment in the Mathematics Classroom*, 1993 Yearbook of the National Council of Teachers of Mathematics, edited by Norman Webb, pp. 229–38. Reston, Va.: National Council of Teachers of Mathematics, 1993.

Kroll, Diana L., Joanne O. Masingila, and Sue Tinsley Mau. "Grading Cooperative Problem Solving." *Mathematics Teacher* 85 (November 1992): 619–27.

Kuhs, Teresa. "Portfolio Assessment: Making It Work the First Time." *Mathematics Teacher* 87 (May 1994): 332–35.

Lambdin, Diana V., and Clare Foresth. "Seamless Assessment/Instruction = Good Teaching." *Teaching Children Mathematics* 2 (January 1996): 294–98.

Lambdin, Diana V., and Vicki L. Walker. "Planning for Classroom Portfolio Assessment." *Arithmetic Teacher* 6 (February 1994): 318–24.

Manon, Jon Rahn. "The Mathematics Test: A New Role for an Old Friend." *Mathematics Teacher* 88 (February 1995): 138–41.

Mayer, Jennifer, and Susan Hillman. "Assessing Students' Thinking through Writing." *Mathematics Teacher* 89 (May 1996): 428–32.

McIntosh, Margaret. "No Time for Writing in Your Class?" *Mathematics Teacher* 84 (September 1991): 423–33.

Merseth, Katherine K., and Joan B. Karp. *Cases of Secondary Mathematics Classrooms*. Cambridge, Mass.: Harvard Mathematics Case Development Project, in press.

Miller, Barbara, and Ilene Kantrov, eds. *Casebook on School Reform*. Portsmouth, N.H.: Heinemann, 1998.

Miller, Barbara, and Ilene Kantrov. *A Guide to Facilitating Cases*. Portsmouth, N.H.: Heinemann, 1998.

Miller, L. Diane. "Begin Mathematics Class with Writing." *Mathematics Teacher* 85 (May 1992): 354–55.

National Council of Teachers of Mathematics. *Assessment Standards for School Mathematics*. Reston, Va.: National Council of Teachers of Mathematics, 1995.

———. "This Is a Test. This Is Only a Test ...." *Mathematics Education Dialogues* 1 (May/June 1998): 1–15.

Norwood, Karen, and Carter, Glenda. "Journal Writing: An Insight into Students' Understanding." *Teaching Children Mathematics* 1 (November 1994): 146–48.

Robinson, Donita. "Student Portfolios in Mathematics." *Mathematics Teacher* 91 (April 1998): 318–25.

Sammons, Kay B., Beth Kobett, Joan Heiss, and Francis (Skip) Fennell. "Linking Instruction and Assessment in the Mathematics Classroom." *Arithmetic Teacher* 39 (February 1992): 11–16.

Schloemer, Cathy G. "An Assessment Example." *Mathematics Teacher* 87 (January 1994): 18–19.

Shannon, Ann, and Judith S. Zawojewski. "Mathematics Performance Assessment: A New Game for All Students." *Mathematics Teacher* 88 (December 1995): 752–57.

Shaw, Jean M., Conn Thomas, Ann Hoffman, and Janis Bulgren. "Using Concept Diagrams to Promote Understanding in Geometry." *Teaching Children Mathematics* 2 (November 1995): 184–89.

Shepard, Lorrie A. "Why We Need Better Assessments." *Educational Leadership* 46 (April 1989): 4–9.

Shimizu, Yoshinori, and Diana Lambdin. "Assessing Students' Performance on an Extended Problem-Solving Task: A Story from a Japanese Classroom." *Mathematics Teacher* 90 (November 1997): 658–64.

Socha, Susan. "Questions with Multiple Answers." *Mathematics Teacher* 84 (November 1991): 638–40.

Stenmark, Jean K., ed. *Mathematics Assessment: Myths, Models, Good Questions, and Practical Suggestions*. Reston, Va.: National Council of Teachers of Mathematics, 1991.

Stenmark, Jean K., Pam Beck, and Harold Asturias. "A Room with More than One View." *Mathematics Teaching in the Middle School* 1 (April 1994): 44–49.

RESOURCES

Thompson, Denisse, Charlene Beckman, and Sharon Senk. "Improving Classroom Tests as a Means of Improving Assessment." *Mathematics Teacher* 90 (January 1997): 58–64.

Tonack, De A. "A Teacher's View on Classroom Assessment: What & How." *Mathematics Teaching in the Middle School* 2 (November-December 1996): 70–73.

Vincent, Mary Lynn, and Linda Wilson. "Informal Assessment: A Story from the Classroom." *Mathematics Teacher* 89 (March 1996): 248–250.

Warloe, Kris. "Assessment as a Dialogue: A Means of Interacting with Middle School Students." In *Assessment in the Mathematics Classroom,* 1993 Yearbook of the National Council of Teachers of Mathematics, edited by Norman Webb, pp. 152–58. Reston, Va.: National Council of Teachers of Mathematics, 1993.

Wilcox, Sandra, and Ronald S. Zielinski. "Using Assessment of Students' Learning to Reshape Teaching." *Mathematics Teacher* 90 (March 1997): 223–29.

Wilcox, Sandra, and Perry Lanier. *Using Assessment to Reshape Teaching: A Casebook for Teachers and Teacher Educators, Curriculum and Staff Development Specialists.* Hillsdale, N.J.: Lawrence Erlbaum Associates, in press.

Zawojewski, Judith S. "Polishing a Data Task: Seeing Better Assessment." *Teaching Children Mathematics* 2 (February 1996): 372–78.

Zawojewski, Judith S., and Richard Lesh. "Scores and Grades: What Are the Problems? What Are the Alternatives?" *Mathematics Teaching in the Middle School* 1 (May 1996): 776–79.

INDEX

RESOURCES

Index

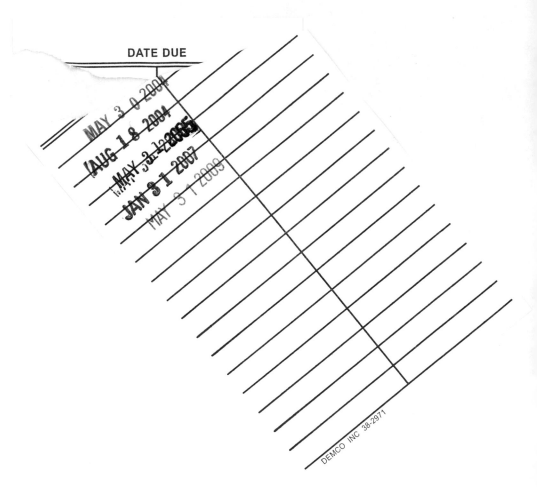

DATE DUE

MAY 3 0 2004

MAY 1 8 2004

AUG 1 8 2004

MAY 3 1 2005

MAY 3 1 2007

JAN 3 1 2007

MAY 3 1 2008

DEMCO INC 38-2971